A Welsh Childhood

Plentyndod Cymraeg

Sam —

I hope you enjoy —

Kathy Sinclair

Love   Kathy

**INTERMEDIA
EDITIONS**

Published in Great Britain by:
Intermedia Editions

An Imprint of:
Intermedia Technology Ltd
PO Box 30, Brighton,
BN45 7BQ, England.

www.intermediaeditions.com

Published 2006

ISBN 0-9552242-0-9

Design and typeset by www.digitalmedialab.co.uk
Printed and bound in Great Britain by Antony Rowe, Eastbourne.

CONTENTS

This book is dedicated to my grandchildren

ACKNOWLEGEMENTS

I would like to express my grateful thanks to Robert McIvor without whose help and support this book would never have been published.

Also my cousin Mari Richards, who was the first to help me fill in the gaps in my father's family.

Kathy Sinclair

Me, aged seven.

CHAPTER ONE

My View of Family Life

My parents were Welsh and I was born prematurely on 11th April 1932 and first saw the light of day in a small private nursing home at 40 Bromley Common in the town of Bromley in Kent. The fee for the privilege of being born in such a place was paid for by my father's uncle Will. At birth I weighed only two and a quarter pounds and it was said you could lose me in a pint jug.

I was transferred to a local hospital where I remained for six weeks. I was lucky to survive because in those days intensive care units did not exist. My mother told me she visited me daily and expressed her milk for me to be fed through a pinhole made in the fine rubber inner tube of a fountain pen, used in the nineteen thirties before ball point pens existed, similar to the cartridge ink pens that children use in this twenty first century. She was twenty one years old, a brown eyed attractive brunette five foot four inches tall with no pronounced accent because she had worked in England for five years and no longer spoke Welsh.

My mother's maiden name was Annie Aucutt Thomas, though my recollection is that everyone called her Ann: she was born in 1911, on what would have been her grandmother Hill's wedding anniversary, had she been alive. Her unusual second Christian name was in memory of her, for Aucutt had been her maiden name. My mother was the only child in her family born with fair hair, the tenth of eleven children all brought up in the Welsh mining village

My mother Annie on the left, with two of her sisters, Addie and Bessie.

of Cymmer, Glamorgan. The family attended The Church in Wales in Glyncorrwg. She had seven sisters: Lizzie, Lillian, Emily, Louisa, Millicent, Beatrice (Bessie) and Adelaide (Addie), and three brothers: Frederick, Charles and Harry. Lillian, Millicent and Frederick all died in early infancy.

My father's name was William Michael Maloney, known in the family as Bill or Willie; when I was born he was twenty five years old: he was five foot nine inches tall and handsome with a ruddy complexion and black wavy hair which stood up on his head. He had the striking blue eyes and the high square forehead of an Irishman but he spoke with a strong Welsh accent and at times his temper was volatile. He was very attractive to women and kept his looks well into his fifties. When I was in my late teens he was physically strong and often mistaken for my boy friend. He was born in the village of Aberkenfig in Glamorgan in 1907 and brought up in the Catholic faith, the second of four children. William, the first born, died in infancy. He had one sister, Winifred Mary, known as Winnie born in 1909 and one brother, Griffith, known as Griff, born in 1920.

Just prior to my birth, my parents lived briefly at 79 Martins Road, Bromley, where my father was a chauffeur. I was christened Kathleen Ann and, because of my surname, throughout my childhood many people believed, incorrectly, that I was Irish.

My father's parents, Kitty and David Moloney, were both aged twenty two when they married in a Catholic ceremony at St Mary House, Bridgend, in 1903. Kitty's maiden name was Edwards, and before she married she was the Post Mistress in Tondu. They went to live at 195 Bridgend Road (which is now number 160), Aberkenfig. My grandfather was a Master Tailor and later in life he be-

3

My grandfather David Maloney centre front at Caterham Barracks in 1915.

came a local councillor and Foreman Tailor at the local mental Institution.

Many years after my father died, David, my much loved husband and I visited my father's brother Griff in Wales, and he showed us a photograph of my grandfather in the uniform of the Welsh Guards taken during the first world war; he died before I was born and I had never seen any photographs of him. To my amazement I noticed that this particular photograph had been taken at the Guards Barracks in Caterham where, by coincidence, we have spent most of our married life. Our son Malcolm, his great grandson, grew up here and attended Caterham School which was founded in Lewisham in 1811 by the Rev. John Townsend, providing a boarding education for the sons of Congregationalist ministers; by 1884 the school had outgrown its premises and the 114 boys with their teaching staff moved from Lewisham to Caterham where in 1890 it opened its doors to the sons of laymen and to day boys. Malcolm was a day boy: I wonder what his great grandfather would have thought about that, and if he liked Caterham when he was a guardsman at the barracks. Another link between them is that Malcolm is at the present time responsible for the mental health of the people of Avon and Wiltshire.

In 2003, after some research I received a letter from the Head-quarters of the Welsh Guards in Wellington Barracks telling me that my grandfather David Moloney enlisted in the Welsh Guards in 1915 at the age of thirty four, but because of his age he was not sent to France: he remained in Caterham until July 1916, when he was transferred to the Reserve Battalion Welsh Guards stationed at the Tower of London, where he remained until he was demobbed in 1919.

My Father's Great Grandparents and their Family. Most of his ancestors were Protestants from South Wales and one branch came from the English border, but his paternal grandfather, Michael Moloney, who was a Catholic emigrated from Youghal in Co. Cork, southern Ireland when he was a small boy; driven out by the Irish potato famine in 1847 which left many starving. Michael married a Welsh girl called Mary Griffiths in Cardiff Register Office on 1st May 1860. He was twenty one years old, a Master Tailor, of 7 St John's Street Cardiff. His father was John Moloney, also a tailor. Mary was twenty two years old and came from the village of Pentyrch in Glamorgan. Her father was Griffith Griffiths who worked as a Baller at the local ironworks. The witnesses at their wedding were David James and Maria Francis.

My great grandparents Michael and Mary Moloney and their dog 'Paddy' outside their home The Holly Bush Inn.

I have a copy of an ancient photograph of my great grandparents taken in the first year of their marriage, standing outside their home, The Holly Bush Inn, Bridgend Road, in the village of Aberkenfig in Glamorgan and behind them on the wall above are the words 'Michael Moloney, Publican'.

Twenty one years later, in the 1881 Census, both aged forty two, Michael and Mary were still living at the Holly Bush Inn and he had become a draper as well as being a tailor, and beer retailer; they had eight children, six boys and two girls. John was a tailor aged 19; William, a butcher, aged 17; Mary, a tailoress, aged 15. Charles W. aged 12, Margaret aged 10, and Joan aged 8 were entered as Scholars. Griffith J. was aged 3 and David M., my grandfather was aged two months born in January that year and the Census had recorded their surname as Moloney. From early childhood my father mistakenly misspelled his surname with an a instead of an o. and always maintained the Irish dramatist George Bernard Shaw once wrote an article in which he said, 'Irish immigrants always found a warm welcome at Mike Maloney's public house in Aberkenfig.'

In February 2004 the Glamorgan Gazette newspaper published a letter from me in which I asked 'Does anyone know what has happened to the Maloney/Moloney family who lived in Aberkenfig in 1881?' For the next week my telephone kept ringing and our local postman brought several letters from the descendants of Michael and Mary Moloney.

Mary Moloney died of influenza and pneumonia at home in April 1901; Michael Moloney died in March 1903 and was buried on St Patrick's day at the church yard in Aberkenfig. My uncle Griff told me my great grandfather had owned a number of properties in the village of Aberkenfig and in 1974 he showed our son Malcolm and me a low wall which was part of a car park, all that remained of the Holly Bush Inn.

Although he had never been to Ireland my father was very proud of his Irish ancestry, until the day in 1973 when he was in central London receiving radiotherapy for prostate cancer, on the very day the IRA attempted to blow up the Old Bailey: that evening as we all watched the news on our television in Caterham, he stood shaking with rage and declared, 'All the b...... Irish should be sent back to Ireland.' Putting my arms around him I told him that with an Irish surname and looking every inch an Irishman, providing he kept his mouth shut, he would be one of the first to be put on a boat.

James William Edwards, my father's maternal grandfather, was born in Much Marcle, Gloucester. He and his brother, whose name

My parents, who were married at Chelsea Registry Office.

I do not know, were apparently fostered out to a farmer in that locality. According to the 1881 Census he was twenty four years old,
working as a Painter and Glazier, and married to my great grandmother Ann, aged nineteen. They had a one year old son, William
Morgan Edwards and were living in Bridgend Road Aberkenfig
with her parents Susan and Thomas Llewellyn, who was a carpenter born in St Brides Minor.

A few months later James, his wife Ann and their son William
moved to 'Sydney Villa' beside the Swan Hotel in Aberkenfig and
James became the village Post Master. In their new home they had
several more children: my grandmother Kitty was first, followed
by one boy, James, and four girls, Mary Adelaide, Emily, Gwenllian and Susan. When she became a widow my great grandmother
Ann Edwards moved out of 'Sydney Villa' and went to live in the
nearby village of Sarn, where family members said she often appeared rather grim looking in her long black dress and hat. Both
'Sydney Villa' and the Swan Hotel are still there in the twenty first
century.

I always called my father's mother Nanny Maloney and her
older brother uncle Will. He was a sports enthusiast; in his youth
he played rugby for Neath and Huddersfield and in 1905 he had a
trial for Wales. At the time of his marriage he was a postman and a
rugby scout for Wales and at the end of the first world war he and
his wife Beatrice known as Beat, moved to London and bought the
Evans Hotel at 9 Euston Square, St Pancras.

They were very fond of my father and called him Willie, and
when he was thirteen he went to live with them in Euston. At the
time they had a baby son, Kenneth Marsden Edwards, known as
Kenny, born in 1920. Later a daughter, Dilys, was born in 1924.

Great uncle Will in rugby kit.

My great uncle and aunt, Will and
Beatrice Edwards and their son
Kenneth.

Uncle Will and auntie Beat had high hopes that when he grew up my father would assist them in running their hotel. Uncle Will owned a large motor car in which he took him to watch rugby at Twickenham and cricket at Lords. My father's sister Winnie told me that when he went home to Aberkenfig with uncle Will he often sported a boater and was full of airs and graces, and thought himself very sophisticated, wearing spats which often hid the fact that he had no socks on.

He became an apprentice house decorator and in his spare time he began to renovate the rooms at the Evans Hotel. He loved going round London in uncle Will's car and learnt to drive when he was still quite young. There was no driving test then and uncle Will had poor eyesight so he often called upon my father to act as his chauffeur; as a result he got to know the streets of London extremely well.

Uncle Will was also interested in motor racing: in 1926 he took my father to meet a friend of his who was attempting a Land Speed Record on Pendine Sands in Carmarthenshire, South Wales. My father told me years later that he was enormously impressed by the occasion, because not only did he meet the racing driver before the event took place, but he also sat on the bonnet of his racing car. I always thought he was talking about Sir Malcolm Campbell, but recently I recalled he said that the following year, when a second attempt was made at the Land Speed Record, the racing car ran out of control and crashed into the sand dunes in Pendine and the driver was killed, which upset uncle Will. The car remained buried until 1969, long after uncle Will's death, when to my father's astonishment, it was dug up and restored.

After doing some research I have discovered the racing driver was a Welshman called John Parry Thomas who for several years had been the Chief Engineer for Leyland Motors and enjoyed testing their luxury cars before delivery. With some misgivings they allowed him to test the last one on the Brooklands racing circuit and he enjoyed the experience so much that he resigned the job with Leyland and moved to a cottage at Brooklands. Shortly after doing so he bought a racing car from the estate of Count Zborowski, a racing driver who had been killed at Monza in 1924. He christened it 'Babs' and it was in this car that he lost his life.

On Sunday mornings in his teens and early twenties my father frequented Speakers Corner in Hyde Park, near Marble Arch in London, where crowds still gather today and speakers are free to express their views on any topic. His sister Winnie told me that when he was young she had seen him get up on a soapbox there and voice his strong socialist belief, which he began to develop then and retained for many years.

When Nanny Maloney's youngest sister Susan got married she and her husband Len Richards went to live in the village of Sarn, a mile from Aberkenfig. They were members of the Labour Party and admired Ramsay MacDonald, Britain's first Labour Prime Minister, so much that they named their first born son Derek Mac-Donald Richards in honour of Ramsay MacDonald.

In March 1926 the government set up a Royal Commission to look into the problems of the Mining Industry. One recommendation was that the miners' wages, which were already low, should be reduced even more. At the same time the mine-owners published new terms of employment, which included another reduction in wages and an extension of the seven-hour working day and the Government said that if the miners did not accept their new terms

My Dad as a boy.

Kenny and Dilys outside Evans hotel.

Grandfather David Maloney on left with brother Griffith.

My grandfather David Maloney with my Dad and his sister Winnie.

of employment they would be locked out of the pits.

Consequently the Trades Union Congress met on 1st May that year and two days later declared a General Strike in defence of the miners' wages and hours, and decided to bring out workers in other key industries to support them, including transport workers, dockers, printers, builders and iron and steel workers, in all a total of three million men which was a fifth of the adult male population of Great Britain. Tremendous efforts were made to reach an agreement with the Government and the mine-owners. The Strike lasted for nine days and for several months after that the miners held out, but by October that year hardship forced them to return to the mines because they and their families were starving. All this happened six years before I was born. 1926 has gone down in British history as The Year of the General Strike.

At the time my grandfather David Maloney was a Labour councillor in Bridgend and because he was outspoken about what he considered the shabby treatment of miners he sometimes needed police protection when leaving council meetings: meanwhile my father aged nineteen was beginning to make a living as a painter and decorator, but his heart was really behind the wheel of a motorcar and he decided he wanted to become a chauffeur. He discussed it with his uncle and aunt and with reluctance they introduced him to Sir Edward Rudd, who needed a chauffeur. My father was pleased to accept a job with him and thoroughly enjoyed it and by 1929 he was well established in this position, driving the latest Packard limousine round London for him. It was a grand car in maroon. However, In 1931 Sir Edward Rudd, of whom I know nothing, decided to emigrate to Argentina and he asked my father to accompany him, but as he had just fallen in love with my mother and did not want to take her away from her family, he said goodbye to Sir Edward and was forced to find another job as a chauffeur.

At the beginning of October uncle Will's son Kenny, then an eleven year old schoolboy, appeared at breakfast one morning complaining of severe stomach ache: my father, who was very fond of his young cousin, offered to drive him to Great Ormond Street Hospital for Children where, he said, he would get immediate treatment, but auntie Beat insisted on calling their doctor first, and by the time Kenny got to hospital it was too late and he died of peritonitis on 4th October 1931. Uncle Will and aunt Beat were devastated by the tragedy.

My grandparents travelled up by train from Aberkenfig to attend Kenny's funeral and soon after returning home my grandfather, David Maloney, collapsed in a coma, and died on 6th November at the age of fifty, which added to the family's grief. Uncle Will accompanied my father and his sister Winnie, and together with my mother, Ann, they went to the funeral in Aberkenfig. Afterwards uncle Will offered my father a partnership in the Evans Hotel but either he was not interested because he was about to get married to my mother or he played his cards badly, for he turned the offer down.

During these events my mother was working as a parlour maid in Wellington Square in Chelsea and she married my father very quietly in Chelsea Registry Office in early December 1931 in the presence of my father's friend Larry Stone and my mother's sister Bessie Thomas.

Great uncle Will in rugby kit in 1901.

Dad aged 23 years.

CHAPTER TWO

My Mother's Maternal Ancestors

Her parents were James and Emily Thomas, née Hill. Emily's great grandfather was John Hill, a Cabinet Maker who lived in Pipe Lane, Hereford; his son, Emily's grandfather Henry Hill, was a Waterman ferrying coal on the river Wye. He married Harriet Howard in the parish church of St John in Hereford. They had two sons, Harry, born in 1842 at Pipe Lane and Frederick, Emily's father, born in 1845 at Martins Street, Hereford.

Emily's uncle Harry Hill became an engine driver and was reputed to have driven one of the first steam locomotives across the famous Crumlin Viaduct, carrying a full load of coal from south Wales. The Viaduct erected in 1857, was made entirely of wrought iron with eight girders. It was the biggest in Great Britain and a remarkable Victorian monument of ingenuity and skill. It stretched across a gorge over 230 feet deep, connecting two mountain tops, and attracted thousands of visitors from all parts of the world: over a hundred years later it was considered unsafe and in 1964 scenes for the film 'Arabesque' starring Sophia Loren and Gregory Peck, were shot on it, even as it was being dismantled.

Emily's father, Frederick Hill (my great grandfather,) showed such academic promise as a boy that his grandfather, John Hill the Hereford cabinet maker, paid for his education. In the 1861 census Frederick was a pupil teacher, living in Whitchurch Doward near Symonds Yat with Susan Aucutt aged sixty five. She introduced him to her granddaughter Elizabeth, who also lived in Whitchurch with her parents Thomas and Sarah Aucutt. Elizabeth's father was a hurdle maker and she was one of seven children, with three brothers: Thomas, James Thelonius and Samuel, and three sisters: Sarah, Mary and Emily. Sometimes the parish clerk at Whitchurch records their baptisms under the name of Alcock, as possibly he was hard of hearing.

Seven years later on 2nd January 1868 Frederick and Elizabeth were married at her parish church in Whitchurch on the banks of the river Wye. He was twenty two and she was twenty four. He was by then a qualified National School Master, Class One, living and working in Bedwelty, Monmouthshire and she lived at home with her parents. One witness at their wedding was Julia Ann Morgan, who lived with Elizabeth's grandmother.

My mother's sisters often told me the Aucutt family came from France. I have tried hard to find a link, without success. According to French friends the name Aucutt does not appear in the French telephone directory.

In the summer of 1869 when Frederick and Elizabeth Hill had been married for just over eighteen months, they left the lovely Wye valley for the Upper Afan Valley in Glamorgan, South Wales, where Frederick had been appointed Master of a new National School in the village of Glyncorrwg, on land donated by a local farmer, Rees Jenkins, where his forebears, also called Rees Jenkins, had lived for several generations. This particular Rees Jenkins had become a rich man from leasing mineral rights to develop coal mines and land to build houses for miners: consequently he had become known as the local Squire and employed a governess to educate his children; he was also one of the managers of the

Great grandparents Hill with their family,
my grandmother Emily is standing beside her mother.

Glyncorrwg National School Board, which was supported by the Diocese of Llandaff together with donations from the local community.

In past centuries the Afan valley like all the valleys in Glamorgan had been a collection of small hamlets making a living with cattle and sheep on the sparsely covered green mountains. Now it was what lay beneath these mountains that attracted hundreds of newcomers, transported on the new railways by modern steam engines. Consequently great tracts of the land had been sold off for mining and railway lines and rows of terraced houses were being constructed to accommodate the rising population who kept coming to Glamorgan, seeking work in the coal mines: and schools were required to educate their children.

In Loving Memory of

FREDERICK HILL,

(OF GLYNCORRWG)

For 27 years Head Master of Glyncorrwg Schools,
Who died on the 27th of May, 1896.

AGED 51 YEARS.

And was interred at Glyncorrwg Churchyard.

Memorial Card for my great grandfather Hill.

When Frederick and Elizabeth got off the train at Glyncorrwg to begin their new life it was a totally different world that confronted them: the noisy railway terminus surrounded by mountains dominated the centre of the village and through a haze of smoke from the steam engines and dank polluted air they could just see the coal tip and the thriving local colliery which employed most of the men in the surrounding district. With the taste of coal dust in their mouths they made their way through the narrow streets, where many friendly young women greeted them in Welsh, holding their babies swaddled in large blankets which were then wrapped around their own bodies. The vicar, standing in St John's church porch, beckoned them into its quiet interior and told them how much their arrival meant to the community, and in what manner life had changed with the constant arrival of men, seeking work, mining for the black gold.

My great grandmother Elizabeth Catherine Thomas.

Great grandfather Charles Thomas.

They then made their way to their new home in a terrace called Lower Stone Row and later went to meet Mr Rees Jenkins at the door of the new National School, which adjoined the church. It consisted of one large room, containing eight long wooden benches, a large slate board, chalk, writing slates and a central stove. My great grandfather Frederick Hill was instructed to keep a school log book, and told that it was his responsibility to ensure that all the children were taught in English. But within a few years he and my great grandmother and all their children, including my grandmother Emily, spoke Welsh like natives.

On his first day as Master of the school, approximately one hundred children registered, with ages ranging from five to thirteen. Fortunately the average attendance was well below that figure. Frederick found the pupils were extremely unruly with a total lack of discipline. Parents were required to pay a penny or two a week for every child attending the school and he had one assistant, a female trainee pupil teacher, by the name of Rachel Plummer. One of the miners informed him that his son working in the local coal pit could earn a lot more money than the salary of a pupil teacher.

The first predicament that confronted Frederick was one of communication for many of the children were Welsh speaking. He divided them into groups and enlisted the aid of the older children to supervise the infants, which was a difficult task with all pupils and staff in one room. So began my great grandfather's life as Master of the Glyncorrwg National School.

To assist the pupils to learn their three Rs, after some months Frederick asked for the schoolroom walls to be whitewashed and oil lamps were installed, to give more light. Some pupils had a long walk to school each day and when the weather was cold the stove

Lizzie Kilner telling me the family history.

was lit. When it rained, which was often, those children that were wet were allowed to sit round it to dry their clothes. One pupil from Cymmer had to walk a distance of three miles, as that village had no school then and when this particular pupil grew up he became Sir William Jenkins, chairman of the Glamorgan Education Authority and later MP for Neath.

Condensation was a problem and the local colliery manager agreed to pay for ventilators to be installed at either end of the school room, and from time to time the vicar's attention was drawn to the state of the closet, outside! Frederick encouraged the pupils to attend regularly and if they arrived late too many times, the school door was locked to keep them out, in order to teach them a lesson. Elizabeth worked part time, taking the girls in sewing lessons, and she was occupied giving birth to five children. Two boys,

Harry (who was born blind) and Frederick, and three girls, Susannah, Emily - my grandmother, born in 1874 - and Louisa.

In 1876 the increasing population in Glyncorrwg put pressure on the School Board to expand, and a small schoolroom was built off the main building to accommodate infants. Frederick was dedicated and hard working and was given another assistant and two pupil teachers and he introduced evening classes for the miners. In the 1881 Census he and Elizabeth and their children were still living in Lower Stone Row, but shortly afterwards, they moved to a larger property in Baxter Terrace.

Frederick was delighted when he heard that a School Board had been set up and that they planned to build separate Board Schools for Boys, Girls and Infants, to provide for the ever growing number of children, but one day in 1885, when the new premises were near completion, he was informed that he and his staff were to be given Three Months' Notice. However, the vicar and Squire Rees Jenkins, who was now a manager of the Board Schools, were instrumental in ensuring that this did not occur, and instead, to the delight of the local population, Frederick and his staff were transferred to the new Glyncorrwg Boys' Board School. Though much relieved at the turn of events, he was sad to leave the old National School building which was so full of memories; it was used as a Sunday school well into the twentieth century.

On a visit to Glyncorrwg in 1980 we were exploring the ruins of the old school when we met a very elderly resident of the village sitting on the church yard wall, who told me, 'When your great grandfather Frederick Hill was headmaster here, I have been told it was not uncommon to see children going home from school with a board tied to their backs saying, 'I Must Not Speak Welsh.'

Great great aunt Ance Aucutt.

Frederick lived long enough to see the birth of at least one of his grandchildren and in May 1896 after a short illness, lasting only a couple of weeks, he died at the age of fifty one, and his wife Elizabeth died a few years later. They are both buried in Glyncorrwg churchyard.

My Mother's Paternal Ancestors. My mother's father, James Thomas had great grandparents by the name of Hopkin and Elizabeth Rees née Morgan. They were married in Neath in 1810 and Hopkin recorded the names of their many offspring in their large Family Bible. He states that in eighteen years of marriage he and his wife Elizabeth had eleven children, ten daughters, and one son called Rees. Hopkin must have been a Royalist because he wrote in his Bible that 'Jennet Charlotte Rees our fifth daughter was born on Nov. 8th 1817 and christened on the night that Princess Charlotte the Princess of Wales was buried' (Charlotte being the only child of King George IV of Great Britain and Ireland and heir to the throne, died in childbirth). In 1828 Hopkin's wife Elizabeth died in childbirth of twin girls, who also died on the same day.

My mother's great grandmother was Rachel Rees their sixth daughter: born in 1819, she married John Peters, a druggist, in Neath parish church in February 1840. John's father, William Peters a Neath grocer, and Mary Renoder were witnesses at their wedding.

Rachel and John Peters set up home in New Street, Neath where only three months after they married their first child, christened Elizabeth Catherine, was born in May 1840. She was my mother's grandmother, and she had seven sisters, Mary Rees, Millicent Bailey, Jennet, Anne, Margaret, Caroline, and Edith Ellen and one brother called William who was deaf and dumb: in the early years

My Mother's cousins.

Ben and Ambrose Thomas.

the family moved to Cwmafan, Merthyr Tydfil and Dowlais and the children were born in different parts of Glamorgan. They finally settled back in the village of Cwmafan, where my mother's great grandfather John Peters died in 1860. In the 1861 census his widow Rachel Peters was head of her household with four daughters, and her son William living with her. William died in Cwmafan in 1892, at the age of 49 years and like his father John Peters and many of my mother's family lies buried in Michaelstone church yard, in Cwmafan.

It is said in the family that my mother's grandmother Elizabeth Catherine Peters and her sister Millicent were adopted by an uncle who was either a surveyor or a lawyer in Neath and that he paid for their education at Cheltenham Ladies' College. But I have no proof because the Ladies' College say they did not keep records in those early days.

However, in 1860 'Squire' Rees Jenkins and his wife did employ Elizabeth Catherine as a Governess for his children Gwen, Mary and Jenkin in his large farmhouse at Ynyscorrwg in the Afan valley. She lived there in some style, for the Squire had house maids, a dairy maid and farm servants. In 1863 at the age of twenty three she relinquished her post as governess to her sister Millicent, to marry William Davies at Blaengwrach chapel of ease, attached to the parish of Glyncorrwg. The quickest and easiest way for her to reach Blaengwrach chapel on her wedding day was on horse back, because it was just over the mountain from the village and she was an excellent horse woman. The mother of one of my cousins said funerals also took place at this chapel and the coffins were carried over the mountain by men who changed hands every so often! Elizabeth Catherine and William Davies had three children,

Rachel, John and Mary and were very happily married for four years until he was killed in a railway accident and I have been told that John and Mary died in childhood.

In 1870 my mother's grandfather Charles Thomas was a thirty nine year old bachelor, working as a waller in Glyncorrwg after being a carrier for some years with his two brothers, travelling through the vale of Glamorgan with a horse and cart, selling cattle fodder and farm produce grown on their grandfather John Thomas' farm in Cowbridge, south Glamorgan, where they were born and grew up: he fell in love with Elizabeth Catherine Davies, who had been a widow for three years.

She had first met him when she was 'Miss Peters the Governess' at Ynyscorrwg farmhouse and he was the carrier delivering farm produce there. Every one called him Charles bach, because he was very small of stature: 'bach' is the Welsh word for 'small.'

One of the brothers of Charles bach, was John Thomas who became the owner of Shelf Farm in Coychurch, Glamorgan. He married twice, and his second wife, called Jennet, bore him two children, a boy named John and a girl named Ethel. John Thomas also owned a pub in the village of Coychurch called the White Horse and he and his two wives are buried in the churchyard there. Charles bach's other brother, whose name I do not know, became the Station Master at Treherbert on the new steam railway.

My mother's grandparents, Charles Thomas and Elizabeth Catherine Davies, were married on 27th May 1870 in Glyncorrwg parish church and my mother's other grandparents, the School Master Frederick Hill and his wife Elizabeth, were witnesses at their wedding. The following year Charles gave up walling and became a collier looking after pit ponies in the local coal mine. Like the

Hills, they began their married life in Stone Row, where Elizabeth Catherine assisted by Rachel Davies, her daughter from her first marriage, opened a Private Venture school. Children were paid for in cash or kind. Cash was 2d weekly. When Rachel grew up she married John Phillips and they had several children. Their second daughter born in 1891 was named Elizabeth Catherine after her grandmother, and was known as Lizzie. She married John Kilner from Trawsfynydd in 1913.

In the late nineteen seventies my husband David and I began to take an interest in our family history and my mother's sister Bessie took us to meet Lizzie Kilner who was in her eighties, living with her daughter Mair. She was a wonderful old lady whom we felt privileged to know. She lived for one hundred and two years of age and had such a good memory. She was able to tell me many things about my mother's paternal ancestors. I feel as if I met them all. My mother's youngest sister Mary also had a very good memory and told me many things about my mother's maternal ancestors.

My great grandmother Elizabeth Catherine Thomas was by all accounts very skilled at embroidery and a wonderful pastry cook and cake maker; she sometimes took herself off to Bath to visit her uncle, for a whole month. She had the demeanour of a grand lady and she liked to dress up in the evenings wearing fine clothes and jewellery and was known to her many grandchildren as 'Mamgu Charles' or Grandmama Charles.

She and Charles Thomas had eight children. My mother's father James , their first child, was born in 1871. He had four sisters: Ellen Jane, Catherine known as Katie, Bessie and Gwenllian, and three brothers: William, David and Thomas. In 1878 Charles gave up looking after the pit ponies and became the parish clerk and sexton of Glyncorrwg Church and Churchyard. Elizabeth Catherine's mother often visited them by steam train. As the family increased in size they eventually moved to Baxter Terrace and when they reached the age of thirteen all the boys became miners at the local colliery and learnt to play the piano at home. My grandfather James played the piano in Glyncorrwg church, until the day when he had an altercation with the vicar and from then on he attended the local Methodist church instead, and played the piano there.

In their old age Charles and Elizabeth Catherine had their photographs taken. She was reputed to be very upright of carriage and in her photograph she certainly looks it; Charles bach's photograph shows he had an enormous white beard and for many years his youngest daughter Gwenllian possessed a portrait of him taken from that photograph. In 1902 at the age of seventy one he died of a brain tumour.

His son James, my mother's father, was always easily recognised because of his very red hair. In 1893 he married Emily Hill at Glyncorrwg parish church; she was eighteen and he was twenty two years old. His family were Welsh speaking and Emily's father, Frederick the School Master, and her sister Susan were witnesses at their wedding.

My mother's parents set up home in one of the new houses built for miners in Cymmer, at 21 Lloyds Terrace, and during the next twenty years at regular intervals, almost like clockwork, Emily gave birth at home to their eleven children; they were all baptised at the parish church in Glyncorrwg, where she and James and both sets of their parents are now buried.

My grandfather James was reputed to be a man of tremendous restless energy and it did not take him long to realise the appalling

One of my grandfather Thomas'
brothers.

One of my Mother's many cousins
on St David's Day.

conditions under which he and his fellow miners worked, so he joined the Miners Union, eventually becoming its leader and getting about on a bicycle, attending frequent meetings. For several years he worked hard attempting to improve the conditions under which they all worked, but as a result he was unpopular with the mine owner and finally lost his job. In his spare time James kept a number of pigs at the top of his garden to feed his large growing family.

Because he died when she was only three and a half years old, my mother had only two recollections of him: seeing him covered in coal dust bathing in a tin bath tub in front of a blazing coal fire in their living room; and of the day she buried her head under pillows on her bed, to shut out the sound of a poor squealing pig he slaughtered at the top of their garden. He died in September 1914, at the comparatively early age of forty three, just before the start of the First World War. My mother's sister Bessie told me that her fourteen year old sister Louisa was stricken with grief and died of meningitis three months later.

My grandmother Emily Thomas was left a widow at the age of forty one with several young children to feed, making the following two or three years financially difficult. The family often went hungry and could not have survived without the help of my grandparents' families like my grandfather's brother Thomas, a farmer in Wick, who often arrived on their door step in Lloyd Terrace with a basket of eggs: the only presents Father Christmas brought my mother and her brothers and sisters during their school years were an orange and a bar of chocolate. There was no Income Support or Family Allowance in those days.

In 1916 after two years as a widow Emily married her first cous-

Great grandparents Hill with his staff at the entrance to Glyncorrwg school.

Cousin Jennifer with me behind the grave of our grandparents and their daughter Louisa, while looking at our great grandparents grave stone.

in Frederick Hill, a widower from Gloucester who was the son of her father's brother Harry, the engine driver. Therefore Emily, who was born a Hill, died a Hill. Frederick, who was also a miner, did not speak Welsh. They continued to live in Lloyds Terrace and just after their wedding her youngest child, three year old Addie, developed rheumatic fever: the family doctor was hastily summoned, but said that he could do nothing, He said 'Just love her, she has not long to live.' However, he was wrong, because Addie lived well into her eighties.

My grandmother, Emily Hill as she had now become, went on to have two more children, William, known as Bill in 1917 and Mary Louise in 1919. When she became pregnant with her at the age of forty six, her second daughter, twenty one year old Emily, married and living in the next village of Abergwynfi, was pregnant with her first baby, my cousin Peggy.

In 1918 after winning the First World War, Great Britain was supposed to be 'A Land Fit for Heroes', but the truth was that when the soldiers returned to civilian life, there was little or no work for many of them and in particular, the miners throughout Great Britain suffered a number of pay cuts

My mother Annie and her brothers and sisters grew up at this time, attending school in Cymmer. They were taught in English, learning writing and arithmetic on slates. She and her sisters Bessie and Addie, who were nearest her in age, wore a clean white pinafore over their dresses on school days: they also wore black leather boots provided by the State. After school, Bessie and my mother often walked to Glyncorrwg to see their many cousins, several of whom became school teachers. She was a bright pupil and won a scholarship, but her stepfather, a miner on a pay cut, could not afford to keep her at school, so she went into service: in those days practically the only job open to girls from large families with limited education.

Her brother Harry who was three years older became a miner when he left school: in 1929 during the slump in the mining industry in south Wales, he followed many others from his colliery seeking work in the mines of Kent. However, he was obviously a late arrival and when he applied they had no more vacancies. Instead he worked as a Porter at Sherrin's Hotel in Cliftonville near Margate, married a local girl and remained there until the second world war.

In the late 1980's, long after Gran Hill had died, David and I went to the village of Glyncorrwg, to visit two of my mother's cousins, brother and sister Ambrose and Dorothy Thomas, neither of whom had ever married and still spoke to each other in Welsh. They were in their eighties and lived together in a little terraced house in Melyn Street. Dorothy played the piano at home, and also in church. That day Ambrose, who had a good tenor voice, stood beside her at their piano and sang 'The Flower Song' from Bizet's opera 'Carmen'. Afterwards he gave us a tour of the village and showed us the two houses in Baxter Terrace where my maternal great grandparents and their families had lived, and the parish church and graveyard where so many of my ancestors are buried; and we made another inspection of the ruins of the National School, where my great grandfather had been Headmaster. When we reached home David presented me with a stone he had picked up among the ruins and ever since we have used it as a door stop.

On a beautiful sunny afternoon in 1996, on our way home after yet another trip to Wales, we visited the little church of St Dubris-

1996. David and me at St. Dubriscious church where my great grandparents
Hill were married in 1868.

cius, at Whitchurch, near Symonds Yat on the banks of river Wye, where my great grandparents Hill were married on a cold January day in 1868. I sat on a bench near the church porch absorbing the atmosphere and dreaming of the time when their wedding took place and my eyes were drawn to the trunk of the tree under which I was sitting, on which lay a broken cross from a nearby tomb stone: to my utter amazement I read the names of my great great grandparents Thomas and Sarah Aucutt. Later I spoke to the church sexton who was working nearby and he said 'There are many Aucutts buried here,' and indeed the first grave stone on the left of the lych-gate is of a Samuel Aucutt.

CHAPTER THREE

My Childhood.

Six weeks after my birth, my mother took me home from hospital to a flat on the first floor of a small house in Shortlands, Bromley. In 1986 David and I discovered it still standing in a street where most had been replaced by modern flats. At the bottom of the back garden was a public house. It must have been there in 1932. My Dad liked his glass of beer!

When I was three months old my father returned to his job as a painter and decorator and we moved to a flat in an Edwardian house in Bartholomew Road, Kentish Town, which was destroyed by the German airforce during the second world war. A few months later we moved to a recently built terraced house in north west London, within walking distance of Hendon Central Underground tube station, which we shared with my father's sister, Winnie. I can vaguely recollect my mother's brother, Charlie, following me round that house as I moved about the floor on my bottom, wearing a nappy and not the disposable variety, for they did not exist. He worked with my father painting and decorating houses and he must have been impressed by the amount of 'decorating' I was doing which he had to clear up! On my second birthday I was lifted into a chair to have a studio photograph taken with a doll I called Bessie. Several of my aunts told me it was because I was so small at birth that I did not walk until I was two years old.

However, there is another possible explanation, for years later

Me at two years with 'Bessie' doll.

at the age of seventeen I started nursing at the Royal National Orthopaedic hospital, in Stanmore, Middlesex: after a very short time
on the wards I developed extremely painful feet. A specialist at
the hospital told me he thought I had had polio as a baby, and I
received a short course of electric shock treatment to the soles of
my feet, which cured me; and on reflection my father admitted I
was ill for a number of weeks during my second year.

My first clear memory was seeing my baby brother just a few
hours old, being held in my Mummy's arms. My mother's sister
Bessie who was a nurse took me by the hand to my parents' bedside at 183 Colin Crescent, London NW9 on 27th September 1934.
Bessie laughed as she pulled back the covers, to show me how to
tell the difference between girls and boys. My mother told me his
name was David Terrence. I was two and a half years old.

I was unaware of the drama of his birth, for my mother, suffering from what she thought was indigestion when in fact she
was in labour, had swallowed turpentine which my father used
for paint stripping in his job. He had put some of it in what had
been an empty bottle of indigestion mixture and after drinking it
she became ill. He was at home that day, together with Bessie, and
realised what had happened; and it was only through her quick
intervention, with her nursing experience, that my mother and my
baby brother lived to tell the tale.

He was called Terry and he was baptised in the local Catholic
church. There were two or three nuns in black habits present on
the day of his baptism, but I do not know where it was, or why they
were there!

At the time Bessie was a nurse in a small hospital in Swiss Cottage which has since been demolished: she and my Dad's sister

Me and baby Terry in back garden at Colindale in 1935.

Winnie were the same age, very good friends, and spent their free time together, laughing and joking. Winnie worked for her uncle at the Evans Hotel in Euston and when Terry was a babe in arms Bessie and Winnie sometimes slept together in our dining room on a collapsible leather bed-settee, activated by a spring. One morning my Dad crept in while they were still asleep, and attempted to fold up the bed by releasing the spring: a lot of screaming took place, accompanied by hysterical laughter, as I and my Mummy rushed in to see the bed folding with them inside. On another occasion, I recall seeing them jigging on the top of the dining-table while singing at the top of their voices: in his old age my Dad told me my mother was beautiful and Bessie was the prettiest of her sisters.

Once, when Gran Hill came on a visit, my parents gave up their

Uncle Charlie's wedding to May. My mother is standing beside him and I am the smallest bridesmaid.

comfortable bed to her and they slept on the bed settee in the dining room, with Terry's cot by the French window. One cold morning I sat beside the sitting room fire with Gran and uncle Charlie, who was holding baby Terry when he accidentally dropped him into the grate. My baby brother was covered in coal dust but otherwise unharmed. When Gran Hill bent to pick him up she joked that he was the grandson of a miner. Later that day she and auntie Bessie took me to the circus in London. I loved the elephants and the clowns.

Terry had an enormous perambulator which my mother used when she took us shopping in Hendon Central. At home we had an adorable kitten and when Terry learnt to crawl, the kitten was

47

forced to hide under the kitchen cabinet because he persisted in tormenting it. One weekend we had so many visitors on a sunny day that my Dad produced a camera and we all gathered in the back garden for a group photograph. Afterwards Terry picked up our pet tortoise and threw it in the air, which made me cry, but he was only a toddler at the time and did not know what he was doing. As we grew older we often played outside in the quiet street with the boy who lived next door, David Butler, in his large toy motor car.

By the time my parents married, Oswald Moseley MP was building up his black shirt Fascist party and holding raucous meetings in east London, some of which my Dad attended out of curiosity. When Terry and I were growing up he liked to discuss politics with us and told us how he once hid in an alley way watching police dealing with thugs who were rioting at one of the meetings, and he said that he thought Oswald Moseley was a charismatic speaker but a misguided politician.

By the age of seven I had been four times a bridesmaid, wearing beautiful dresses which I loved. The first time was at uncle Charlie's wedding to May Bull when I was two and a half years old. The only recollection I have of their wedding day is that as we left the churchyard someone threw rice confetti which stung my arms and legs and made me cry!

On the 6th May 1935, when I was just three years old, I had fun travelling on the London Underground with my aunts Winnie and Bessie. I clearly recall them holding me tight when I was frightened by the thunderous sound of an approaching tube train, accompanied by a strong draft of air as it emerged from the tunnel and stopped with doors opening and shutting automatically. Between

Me at two and half years of age.

My mother holding her sister
Bessie by the arm.

Dad and me on the back garden steps of Evans hotel in 1935.

Terry and me with my mother on the front doorstep in Colindale.

them my aunts carried me up the escalator to the street above and held me up high among the cheering crowds somewhere near the Mall, so that I could see King George and Queen Mary go by in a state coach to celebrate their Silver Jubilee.

That summer our little family went to Wales by steam train to see Gran Hill and our step grandfather Fred, long since retired and known to one and all as 'Pop'. Gran's sister Louie was there on a visit from Liverpool with her dog, a Pomeranian with white silky hair. My Dad took a photo of Mummy, Terry and me with Pop at the front door of their home. At bed time I was lifted up to kiss him goodnight as he sat in his carver chair and his large moustache tickled my face. Gran, a large lady, was gradually losing her sight and next day she came on the train with us to Burry Port in Carmarthenshire to visit her eldest daughter Lizzie and her hus-

51

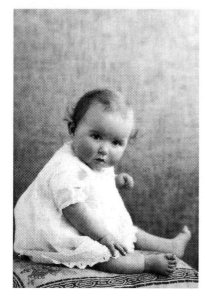

Me at eight months.

My mother's cousin Freddie with
Mummy and baby Terry.

band Jim Ogborn. There I walked hand in hand with her picking runner beans in auntie Lizzie's large garden.

When I was young I was blessed with extremely curly hair and as was the fashion of the time my clothes were like those worn by the little film star Shirley Temple. My mother took me to see one of her films when I was about three years old: I had never been in a cinema before and as we walked in I saw her on the screen and just for a moment I thought I was looking in a mirror.

In 1936 I was a bridesmaid at Winnie's wedding to a carpenter, Arthur Cole. Sadly I have little recollection of it and years later she told me her wedding took place in the local parish church in Colindale, because uncle Arthur was not a Catholic. When our son Malcolm was a lad my aunt Addie gave him a photograph of me taken that day and said, 'This is the prettiest little bridesmaid I ever saw.' I think she was biased! Unfortunately fifty years later when Winnie and Arthur celebrated their Golden Wedding day I was ill and unable to be present.

Pop died in 1936 and my mother went down to Cymmer for his funeral, and Bessie gave up nursing in London and returned to Wales permanently, where she met and married Ron Smith - a family wedding when I was not a bridesmaid. In October that year their first baby called Betty was born: she became a pretty little fair haired girl.

EUSTON SQUARE

On Sunday mornings my Dad often took me by underground tube train from Hendon Central to visit his uncle Will and auntie Beat at the Evans Hotel in Euston Square beside the mainline railway station. On the first occasion I was very frightened by the noise in the tube train and when we emerged into the mainline station

I held my Dad's hand tightly, keeping as close to him as possible, trying to block out the noise made by the enormous steam locomotives there. I was very glad when we passed under an enormous Arch at the entrance to the station, and emerged into the sunshine entering a world far removed from the peaceful life of London suburbia. I loved it, and still love London today. Dad told me that Euston was the first railway station built in Great Britain over a hundred years before, and that all the hotels in Euston Square and round about had been built to accommodate passengers who travelled by train to London from the north of England and Scotland, and that long before he was born the trains were hauled up the hill to Camden Town from Euston by cable and horses. After that first visit I knew what to expect and ever since I have always enjoyed travelling by train.

Many years later when he had a car we drove through London and he showed me the shed in Camden where a century ago the engines were stored. It is still there today in the twenty first century, but is now famous as an arts centre, called the Roundhouse.

The main entrance of the Evans Hotel was up a flight of steps to what appeared to me to be a large front door, but Dad and I always made our way through a wrought iron gate in railings and down some stone steps to the basement to reach a below stairs kitchen. There I sat at a large table drinking pop in front of a kitchen range with a high mantelpiece, while Dad drank tea with and chatted to auntie Beat and uncle Will. Like my father, uncle Will often wore a double breasted suit and a waistcoat on Sunday mornings. He also wore a pocket watch and chain which fascinated me. I always asked him the time so that he would bring it out and look at it and then put it to my ear so that I could hear it ticking. Before mak-

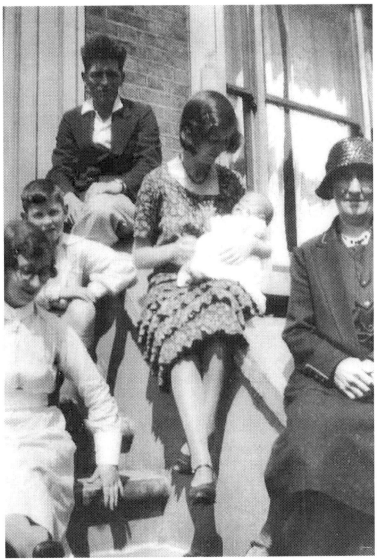

Our home in Kentish Town. L to R - Bessie in nurses uniform, uncle Griff, my parents with me and Nanny Maloney.

Terry and me playing in the road in Colin Crescent.

ing our way home Dad and I usually stopped near the entrance to Euston station, at another hotel, owned by auntie Beat's sister Mary and her husband Oscar Gifford. We were always made very welcome there, too.

Uncle Will was broad shouldered with striking blue eyes and when I was a little girl he drove a large black motorcar. Sometimes he had a chauffeur because his sight was becoming weak and occasionally on a Sunday, with my Dad at the wheel, uncle Will took our little family out for a drive in the country. Once we visited one of his friends, a Mr King who owned a large number of green-

56

houses full of tomatoes. What a wonderful smell they had! Winnie would not have enjoyed it because she did not like tomatoes.

It was fashionable for men to smoke cigarettes and my father was no exception. He began smoking Wills Woodbines in his early teens and was a heavy smoker for most of his adult life. From boyhood he also loved eating sweets, which ruined his teeth. His sister Winnie and my mother always called him Bill.

Auntie Beat, a tall lady with a very distinctive voice, made a great fuss of me and gave me lovely dresses which were the envy of all my friends at birthday parties. Most of my adult life I thought they were cast off clothes which had belonged to her daughter Dilys, but my mother's sister Addie told me in 1995 that auntie Beat bought these exclusive dresses for me at the sales, in the large London department stores of Harrods and Selfridges. They were extremely beautiful and with them I wore white ankle socks and black patent leather ankle strap shoes.

On our Sunday visits to great uncle Will's hotel I was free to wander about and explore the guests' dining room and the parlour on the ground floor at the front of the hotel, in which stood a piano. I enjoyed playing in the small walled garden and occasionally used the antique water closet there. Sometimes I sat on the wrought iron seat on the top of the steps at the front entrance. I remember sitting there wearing a little white pleated skirt, looking out on to Euston Square and eating black cherries on a beautiful sunny Sunday morning. I felt like a princess and ever since I have loved black cherries.

Many years later, in 1971, I accompanied my Dad on a visit to London. For fourteen years he had been living in the African state of Rhodesia, now called. Zimbabwe, during which time we had not met. He had returned unexpectedly from Africa, a sick man with prostate cancer, and together with my stepmother Anne we were in London that day seeking expert medical opinion from a consultant in Harley Street. Afterwards, we took a bus to Euston and as we expected we found the whole area greatly changed, for Euston Square was unrecognisable. The Evans Hotel had been demolished together with all the other hotels in the area, to allow for the vast expansion of the mainline railway station. Even the famous Euston Arch, much loved by the former Poet Laureate John Betjeman, had been removed: and where the Evans Hotel had once stood was an enormous car park. Dad looked around and found a lamp post which he said had stood outside the hotel entrance. He went up to it and gave it a cuddle! It was an emotional moment for both of us.

CHAPTER FOUR

Aerodrome Estate, Edgware

When Winnie and Arthur married they bought the house in Colindale and our parents decided to buy their own home as well. We were transported in a large furniture van to a three bedroom house with a small garden back and front on the new Aerodrome Estate in Edgware, just a mile and a half from Colindale on the outskirts of London. The estate was built on the former Stag Lane aerodrome, which had been occasionally used by the solo air aces of the nineteen thirties, husband and wife Jim Mollison and Amy Johnson. Near the De Havillands aircraft factory, just over half a mile from our new home, was a road named Mollison Way in tribute to them, with a small parade of shops for us to use.

A number of roads on the estate were named after famous British artists. Our house was in Raeburn Road (Raeburn was a Scottish artist). The house had a wonderful new smell and my parents were ecstatically happy to have a home of their own, with a new school close by which I started attending in September 1937. Years later I learnt the house cost £350. Gran Hill loaned them £200 and they took out a mortgage for £150! How times have changed.

The floors throughout our new house were covered in linoleum and rugs with slip mats at every door. A carpet runner ran along the centre of the hall way and up the stairs. The sitting room had a brand new expensive three piece suite, of which my father was extremely proud. It proved to be a good buy because twenty years

Terry and me at the seaside with our Mum.

later that same suite of furniture was re-covered in maroon uncut moquette and placed in the lounge of his new detached house at 15 St James' Avenue, St Peters, in Broadstairs.

The dining room, with a French window, had a new dining table and chairs, the leather bed settee from Colindale and a wireless with just the two channels in existence then, called Home Service and Light Programme. Both living rooms and the two main bedrooms had open fireplaces and art deco lamp shades in the ceiling and all the rooms were decorated with pretty wall paper.

The partially tiled kitchen though small had all the modern conveniences of the time: a gas boiler for washing clothes, a larder, a modern electric cooker of my mother's choice with which she was delighted, and the latest gadget, a Hoover vacuum cleaner, stored in the cupboard under the stairs, for which we had just one power socket. In our back garden there was, of course, a very necessary coal bunker.

On the landing at the top of the stairs was a partially tiled bath room and water closet. In the modern homes at that time there were no fitted carpets, central heating, dish washers, tumble dryers or washing machines; but we did have an airing cupboard in the back bedroom heated from a boiler behind the dining room coal fire. Our parents' bedroom had a new wardrobe, a chest of drawers and a dressing table with three mirrors on which lay a silver vanity set - one of our parents' wedding presents - and a seat on which my mother could sit and titivate herself. I now possess a trinket jar from that vanity set which I keep on my Welsh Dresser. Best of all for Terry and me, we had our own bedrooms.

Most houses were in blocks of four with metal window frames. Our house was slightly more upmarket because it was semi-de-

On the sands at Margate.

tached with a bay windowed sitting room from which we looked
straight down the slight incline of Constable Gardens to the aircraft
factory, about a mile away. Next door lived Mr and Mrs Hall, who
were childless. Mrs Usall, a widow with an Airedale terrier and a
grown up family in an end of terrace house, was our neighbour on
the other side. All the other neighbours had young families, with
whom we quickly became friends.

Cars were rare before the second world war and we children all
played on the flagstone pavement or in the road outside our homes.
Every garden had a gated entrance with a fence and a concrete
path to the front door. Apart from birdsong, an occasional low flying light aircraft or barking dog and of course children at play, it

With our parents watching Punch and Judy on the Isle of Wight.

was a peaceful place to live. In the summertime when the Walls ice cream man arrived ringing a hand bell and shouting 'Stop me and buy one!' play stopped. We would gather round him in the middle of the road with our halfpennies waiting for him to open the large box of ice cream attached to the front of his tricycle.

We always got excited when my mother told us we were going on a visit to Winnie and Arthur's house which meant a walk to Burnt Oak shopping centre to catch a trolley bus along the Edgware Road to Colindale and not long after they married Arthur bought a Border Collie puppy called Betsy and a motor car and one day they all arrived at our front gate. After that we often went out for adventures in their car which was small with four adults, two children and a dog making it a tight squeeze. Of course, there were no seat belts then! Taking a picnic we visited Cannons Park to see

63

Terry and I at the seaside with our Mum and Dad.

the swans on the lake, Windsor Great Park where we saw lots of peacocks, Kew Gardens with wonderful flowers and the hot house where the bananas grew, the London Zoo where a giraffe lifted off my father's hat, or we enjoyed an air display at Hendon Aerodrome, observing them flying while we sat in the car.

SEASIDE HOLIDAYS

Winnie was always a nervous passenger. Once on holiday at the seaside with them, when travelling down a steep hill in Arthur's car, he was forced to stop sharply because she began to panic: terrified we would all end up in the sea. Years later when my father lived in Broadstairs, and I was there they came to stay with us and my Dad took us out for a drive in his car. As we approached the harbour Winnie exclaimed 'Bill, this is the very spot where I lost my head years ago and I think I will do so again if you do not drive very slowly!'

Before the second world war our parents took us on two seaside holidays at boarding houses. One was at the resort of Littlehampton in Sussex, where I recall we all sat on the sands watching Punch and Judy, and one afternoon we took a trip in a large rowing boat when a storm blew up and the sea became rough making everyone seasick and I was very frightened. Ever since I have been nervous at sea and never feel happy in a boat, even on a pond! Our second seaside holiday was spent at Ventnor on the Isle of Wight where we saw some lovely multicoloured sand cliffs at Alum Bay and visited a museum to see a large whale bone and the skeleton of a dinosaur at Blackgang Chine. I really enjoyed our holiday on the Isle of Wight. In 1996 our adorable granddaughter Lydia was born there. My stepmother told me sixty years later that my Dad

65

told her he was able to take us on that particular holiday because he had won some money at the races! All his life he liked to place bets on the horses.

My mother's brother Harry lived with his wife Millie and our cousin John in Margate, a seaside resort in Kent. We often visited them and even as we got off the train with Terry in a pushchair, both of us wearing little white canvas sandals, which my mother cleaned every night with a chalky substance called Blanco, we could taste and smell the sea in the air and became excited as we made our way along the promenade to uncle Harry's house, past the large Dreamland fairground and lots of little shops selling buckets and spades to make sandcastles; while on the beach we could see Punch and Judy and children having donkey rides; all of which made us recognise the treats in store for us. One such sunny day on Margate sands I had my photograph taken by a Sunbeam beach photographer and my mother was later approached by Nestles, who wanted to use me as a model for a chocolate advertisement, but she would not agree to it!

At Easter time in 1937 I was taken to Margate by Mummy's sister Addie and Gran Hill, to stay with Uncle Harry and family. Addie spoiled me and I had a great time playing on the sands with cousin John and even enjoyed walking along the promenade with Gran Hill. Every night I crept into Addie's bed for a cuddle. One night I got a shock when I found my mother there. She was not best pleased at my behaviour. I received a little smack and was sent back to my own bed.

My father, it seems, had plans for my private education at the excellent fee paying North London Collegiate High school for girls in Edgware. But because he had always been somewhat irrespon-

On Margate promenade with Addie and Gran Hill.

Winnie.

sible with money my aunt Mary told me years later that when she heard him say that, she told him 'The only high school that Kathleen will go to is one up on a hill!' How right she was! In the nineties I made a new friend in the jazz world and I discovered she had been a pupil there.

STARTING SCHOOL

My mother made a friend who lived on the estate in Millais Gardens with a son called Peter and we often played together while our mothers talked. One summer day they both looked worried and spoke quietly about something called a 'Crisis'. Peter and I had no idea what it was, but it frightened me to see their anxious faces. In September 1937 Peter and I started school together sitting at single desks with pencils and paper. First thing every morning our teacher asked us to hold up a clean handkerchief for inspection. I bet that no longer happens! I carried mine in a small purse on a shoulder strap which also contained a penny to spend at a sweet shop after school. My teacher was kind and she put stars for good work in our spelling and sum books, and frequently called me out to her desk to admire my frilly knickers and pretty dresses.

One day after school a vendor appeared at the school gate selling adorable yellow baby chicks for a penny. I bought one and ran to my Mum with it, but she was cross and took it straight back to him. We had no pets when we lived in Edgware, except for a goldfish called Sammy who lived only a few weeks.

On wintry days I wore long brown wool stockings or leggings which little girls wore in those days, made of velvet corduroy secured with buttons from ankles to just above the knees; I also wore a rabbit wool hat on cold days which my mother knitted for me with a pointed tip and was called a pixie hat, a fashion of the thirties. At first I loved it, but when I began to complain it made my head itch she would not agree with me: day or so later a nurse came to our school to inspect our heads, and I was given a note to take home to say that I had head lice. Ugh! That was why my head itched, and for several evenings I had to kneel down on the carpet with my head over a large sheet of newspaper while my mother pulled a very fine tooth comb through my curls to get rid of the nits.

Hoping one day to own a car, my Dad constructed a garage made of asbestos beside the house. There he stored the tools, paints and brushes he used in his work, his bicycle, the lawn mower and some of our toys. Because our back garden had no trees to shelter under on a hot day he built a large wooden verandah with a canopy outside our French widow which faced west and was a popular place to sit on sunny afternoons, and aunt Beat bought me a little cane musical chair and a pretty parasol. On hot days I could never understand why grown ups liked drinking tea to cool themselves down. One such day auntie Bessie was sitting there with little Betty while she breast fed her new baby, our cousin Keith. She turned to Terry and offered him some. The verandah shook as he bolted in horror!!!

My mother was an expert knitter and in my first year at school she taught me how to knit and because she helped me with my reading and spelling I was top of the class. She was very fond of books and often sat reading on the verandah. She was an excellent cook and by the time I was six years old she had shown me how to make drop scones and Welsh cakes on the hot plate of her electric cooker. I can still smell them! Thus she instilled in me a life long

Terry and me at Littlehampton.

Me on Margate beach.

interest in reading, knitting and cake making. In those pre-war years she had a lovely complexion in a heart shaped face. She was slim, with a dazzling smile and perfect teeth. I did not know then that it was quite common for most of her generation to have a full set of false teeth by the time they reached their twenties.

I began to suffer from sore throats and in the spring of 1938 I had a tonsillectomy at Great Ormond Street Hospital for Children. My mother held my hand while I was given the anaesthetic and after the operation I was allowed to sit up in bed and eat jelly and ice cream. Later a nurse came and gave me some medicine which tasted so dreadful that when she wasn't looking I threw it on the floor. My mother brought me a present of a china doll wearing a nappy and when I left the hospital clutching it, I stopped to kiss my favourite nurse good-bye and told her that I too would be a nurse one day. When I did become a nurse I always made sure that my patients took their medicine!

In those days children on our estate had lots of freedom and Terry was a mischievous little boy. So that we could come and go at will our back door was never locked when we were out at play. When he was less than four years old he painted our front garden picket fence and his tricycle with vivid coloured paints he found in the garage. He liked cream horn cakes and occasionally we had them as a special treat at tea time. Having eaten them my mother once instructed us 'Do not tell Daddy because there are none left for him.' Guess what was the first thing Terry said when Daddy appeared? He had hardly put his foot in the door!

Every day of the week a milkman with a horse and cart delivered pasteurised milk in pint bottles with cardboard tops to every house in the street. The horse occasionally dropped a dollop of manure and as if by magic someone quickly appeared with a bucket and spade to pick it up for their garden. The baker too carried a basket of bread round the houses and once my mother did not respond to his knock so he left a loaf on our porch window sill, shaded by a lilac tree. Terry and I were outside playing and I saw him pick it up, eat the whole of the centre of it and replace the shell on the sill. I can still see the look of amazement on Mummy's face when she opened the front door to pick up what she thought was a whole loaf of bread.

We had a number of violent storms in north west London in the nineteen thirties, which filled my mother with apprehension: if my father was out she would rush round the house in a panic, turning all the mirrors to the wall and hide the silver and cutlery. Then she would sit on our sitting room settee with Terry and me kneeling either side of her to bury our heads in her lap and feel her tremble. The position of our house provided excellent views of the thunder balls and the lightning, and, years later, of enemy aircraft over London. Dear Winnie was terrified of thunderstorms too and also frightened of spiders. One day a storm was so violent that she hid in the cupboard under the stairs in Colindale; the catch slipped and she remained locked in the cupboard until Arthur returned in the evening. Poor auntie Win! Many years later when my father lived in Africa where electric storms are frequent and violent, he told me that he wrote to her and said, 'Winnie, you would not like it here because the thunderstorms are very severe and spiders as big as saucers live in the cupboards!'

Uncle Arthur's brother Bill and his wife Phyllis also lived in Colindale and they had two daughters: one of my age was named Janet. My mother and Phyllis were friends and before the second world war our families spent a lot of time together. One day in the summer of 1938 we were at their home when there was a commotion in the street outside for King George VI and Queen Elizabeth were about to pass by on a visit to nearby Hendon aerodrome, so we all trooped upstairs and sat looking out of their front bedroom windows to watch them. As they and their cavalcade drove by, my father said, 'King George VI will be our last monarch.' He was wrong!

CHAPTER FIVE

Pre WW2 London Suburban Lifestyle

On the Aerodrome estate before the second world war and in the British population as a whole, it was uncommon for young people to live together openly before marriage: the legal age to marry without parental consent was twenty one and most couples wed at about that age and because the contraceptive pill had not been invented brides quickly became pregnant.

Shops did not open on Sundays in Great Britain then because it was considered a day of rest, except for workers in hospitals, transport and like industries. On the estate where we lived women cooked a Sunday roast dinner usually eaten at midday and families sat round a dining table to eat together and frequently spent summer Sunday afternoons in their gardens, where the sound of many hand driven lawn mowers could be heard (for there was no such thing as an electric mower) and very few motor cars. In the winter after Sunday dinner we sat round an open coal fire in the dining room with our parents and while they listened to the wireless we played with our toys. Only on special occasions or when we had lots of visitors did we use the sitting room or light the fire there.

In those days, before home owners had washing machines, Monday was known as 'wash day' which often took several hours to complete with the use of a wash board, a scrubbing brush, a blue bag, a boiler, and a mangle outside the back door to wring out the clothes before putting them on a straight clothes line held up with a prop. Therefore on Monday evening when the menfolk returned from work a simple meal was provided, like pickles and cold meat left overs from Sunday's joint. A laundry delivery service took care of bed linen and ironing usually took place all day Tuesday! Electric irons were small and basic and there was no such thing as a steam iron. Nothing was drip dry then and housewives wore wrap around pinafores to protect their dresses when doing household chores.

Because nursery schools did not exist children under five remained at home and few mothers went out to work. Every town had a long parade of shops of every sort, now found together in super markets. Prams with babies in them could be safely left outside shop fronts while mothers were inside. All goods were carried home in large shopping bags or on the prams and every item was paid for in cash.

In my childhood years I never saw a man doing the shopping, carrying it home or pushing a pram, though I suppose some men did. It was also unheard of for women to wear trousers before the second world war and very few went bare headed, some wore head scarves but most wore hats and my mother adored them. After the war when women started to go out to work en masse and family cars began to appear on the streets, hats ceased to be so fashionable except for weddings and special events.

Every one walked a great deal more than they do now, so cobblers were kept busy and neighbours were very friendly: everyone passed the time of day. When the Aerodrome estate was built it had no garages as few cars existed. Very few people had a telephone in their home and the only telephone box was in Mollison Way. There was a blue police box in Burnt Oak Broadway, on the Edgware

Road, connected to the local police station which in an emergency, the public could use. Now the only time a police box is seen is in the Children's film or television series about 'Dr. Who'.

Public transport was excellent, with buses from Mollison Way and trolley buses ran along the Edgware Road, and with three tube stations within easy reach many of the menfolk commuted from the estate in double breasted suits, always in muted colours, sometimes pinstriped, their trousers supported by braces. Most wore ties and cotton shirts with detachable collars easily replaced to save washing. Shoes were made of leather. Trainers and jeans had yet to be invented. Long macintoshes were worn and black umbrellas were used in wet weather. Trilby hats were the most popular headgear for men but I seldom saw my father in a hat, possibly something to do with his hair style. He was extremely proud of his dark wavy hair.

HOME LIFE

I do not recall that my mother was ever really cross with us. She was very loving, but strict about manners. We always had to remember our P's and Q's. We ate all our meals at the dining table covered with a table cloth, on which we were not allowed to put our elbows, and we were forbidden to speak with our mouths full. We were encouraged to clear our plates and ask permission to leave the table when we had finished. Sweets were forbidden before lunch and we listened to Children's Hour on the wireless while we ate our tea. We put away our toys at bedtime and said our prayers before going to sleep. Once when we had guests I misbehaved and my mother made me stand in the corner of the dining room with my face to the wall for a few minutes! On another occa-

Uncle Bill.

sion because I did not clear my plate at lunchtime, it was presented to me at tea time. Ugh! But I still did not eat it! Mummy used to say that Terry needed a lot more cuddles than I did. I did not agree but did not tell her; I loved her too much.

As for my father, there was a time when he was cross with me, of which more later, but he was generally loving and kind to us both and I do not remember that he ever smacked us. In the mornings he was sometimes in a very bad temper with my mother and our parents occasionally fell out. One day my Mum sat on a little chair in the dining room reading a book instead of preparing breakfast. Naughty! When my father entered and discovered her, he was so angry that he pulled the chair from under her. After he had gone to work she told me that he had got up on the wrong side of the bed! But they had fun too, and I know she loved him dearly. He liked to tease her and I can hear her laughter yet. My aunts have often said my laugh is exactly the same now. I remember her standing in the kitchen one day screaming in horror. 'Bill! Come quick! There is a mouse in the bread bin!' My father came to the rescue and held up the mouse by its tail so that we could see it was a clockwork toy, which made us all laugh. He told me at the end of his life that he had really loved her.

One day she took me to see 'Snow White', my first coloured film, and afterwards I wouldn't eat red apples for a long time! That summer of 1938 I was bridesmaid at the wedding of my mother's youngest brother Bill and his bride, Kitty. My dress was pink satin with many frills. It was a double wedding: Kitty's sister was getting married that day too. Uncle Bill was twenty two years old, tall dark and handsome, and as he turned and winked at me walking down the aisle behind him and his bride I fell in love with him.

I was thrilled whenever they came to stay with us for a weekend and Terry and I were allowed to stay up late. They always brought Dinda their springer spaniel with them and she slept at the foot of the stairs. At tea time on these occasions uncle Charlie and auntie May who lived nearby and auntie Winnie and uncle Arthur would join us. Afterwards we all played table skittles in the dining room and later we had an unaccompanied sing song. Uncle Bill who had a melodious voice sang the latest ballads and Dad would sing traditional airs standing with his arm resting on our wooden mantelpiece. He always finished with 'I will take you home again, Kathleen'. Without television people managed to entertain themselves quite well.

On Sunday mornings my mother often treated us to a penny stick of chocolate she bought every week from Woolworths, known as the 'Threepenny and Sixpenny Store', placing them at our bedsides when we were asleep on Saturday nights. The intention was that the chocolate kept us quiet on Sunday mornings so that they could have a lie in. Once we had eaten the chocolate and played quietly for a while we would climb into bed with them.

When he was three years old Terry was found to have a turn in his eye and he had to wear glasses with a patch over one eye. He adapted to it well and wore them until he left school. It is an inherited defective gene in our mother's family and many of my first cousins had the same problem in childhood. I was one of the lucky ones. When I was eleven years old I had a fight with a bully boy after school because he called Terry 'four eyes'. That was the only time in all of my school days when I was aware of any bullying.

After our school summer holidays Peter and I moved up a class but our new teacher did not make a fuss of me or inspect my pretty

Terry and me at our front door in Raeburn Road.

clothes! So I played truant, going home at playtime. My mother was out so I sat on the pavement outside our house making mud pies in the gutter until she appeared! Next day I returned to school quite happily.

One day after school I was playing with Peter while our mothers sat drinking tea and Peter's mother was crying. She was telling my mother about a newsreel she had seen at the cinema and I heard the word 'Munich'. Peter and I did not know that they were both worried about what was happening in the world. Only years later did I realise she was talking about our Prime Minister Neville Chamberlain who had returned from a visit to see Adolf Hitler in Munich.

Christmas 1938 is the most clear of all my early childhood memories. My mother took us to Selfridges in London's Oxford Street to see Father Christmas in his grotto full of toys. He asked us what we would like for Christmas and I said I would like a dolls pram and Terry said he would like a tricycle and we promised to be good. I worried about how he would get the toys down our chimney and on Christmas day we woke up to find he had left us a pillowcase full of presents at the foot of our beds. We were thrilled, but there was no pram or tricycle: after a while our parents, remaining in bed, bid us go down stairs to see if Father Christmas was still in the house. We couldn't find him but the sitting room door was wide open, the curtains were closed and the room was all lit up, transformed as if by magic. My father had purchased a large Christmas tree at Burnt Oak market late the night before and it stood near the window festooned with lights and a fairy on the top touching the ceiling; the walls were decorated with balloons and paper chains and above the fireplace hung an enormous Christmas

Addie's wedding guests. L Dad's brother Griff. Tall man in centre is uncle Bill and Nanny is standing between my parents on the right.

cracker. Underneath the tree was a new red three wheeler tricycle and a green doll's pram Father Christmas had remembered!

In 1939 Nanny Maloney and Griff came to stay with us and for a little while Terry and I shared a bed so that they could have the large upstairs front room with two beds. During her stay I went to church with Nanny on Sunday mornings. I have no recollection of going to church before that, except when Terry was baptised.

Nanny was less than five foot tall, a small very slim lady with straight white hair. My father seemed to tower above her. She was very fond of her children, and I think Griff was the apple of her eye at that time. Winnie resembled her somewhat as she grew older, although she never had white hair. When Nanny did any sewing while she was staying with us she always asked me to thread the

Me as a bridesmaid at auntie Winnie's wedding.

needle for her, but I cannot recollect whether she wore glasses. Now I too have difficulty threading a needle and wish my granddaughters lived near to help me; my hair too, is suddenly white, just like Nanny's.

There was thirteen years between my father and his brother Griff. Like all boys of his age Griff had an enormous appetite. He also had a sweet tooth and loved my mother's cakes and any sweets or fruit he found about the house. Nanny put lots and lots of sugar in his tea! We liked him very much. When my father died Griff was in his early fifties and whenever I saw him, though he was a more gentle character, the timbre of his voice and to some extent his appearance reminded me of my father. I found this emotionally disturbing and difficult to cope with and yet, sometimes, strangely comforting.

In April 1939, I became a bridesmaid to my beloved aunt Addie. She was very slim and looked radiant in a long white satin gown; my dress was pink taffeta with small embroidered flowers covered with lace netting and an orange blossom coronet; uncle Bill's wife Kitty was a maid of honour in a long mauve gown. Addie and her groom, Tom Bowen, a Welshman from Burry Port who looked very smart in a new light grey suit, were married in our local parish church. After the ceremony we stood in the church porch for photographs and Mummy, looking elegant in a navy suit with a pretty blouse and one of her fashionable hats, stood watching us with Terry and gently pushed him forward. He was wearing a little grey suit and looked clean and healthy and his face held an angelic expression as he presented a ribboned silver horseshoe to the bride and groom. Uncle Bill, Winnie, Arthur, Nanny and Griff were there too. The wedding reception was held at our home and

Addie and Tom's wedding day where I was a bridesmaid.

my mother worked hard to make it a success. Our house was full of tables with lots of good things to eat and drink. We loved our new uncle who was very athletic and full of fun and what's more, that Easter he had taken us to a chocolate shop in Burnt Oak and bought us both enormous Easter eggs!

At school we celebrated Empire Day in May and I and all the girls in my class wore red white and blue ribbons in our hair and our teacher showed us a huge map of the world, explaining that the many pink areas were part of the British Empire on which the sun never set! I asked her to show me Wales! We then trooped into a hall festooned in red white and blue with a large picture of our King and Queen and a huge Union Jack, there we were entertained by a ventriloquist. We sang lots of songs including 'There'll always be an England' and the National Anthem and I came home with a little Union flag and two sticky doughnuts for our tea!

WAR CLOUDS

At this time my little brother and I were blissfully happy, totally oblivious of the catastrophe looming ahead. There was a shortage of money in our home because living on a new housing estate ten miles from central London meant there was little demand for my father's skill as a painter and decorator and he was often unemployed. But we never went without: sometimes my father went to work at the usual time, hoping my mother would not suspect; but she figured it all out when he kept coming home with bags of groceries from the Evans Hotel, so she took a part time job as a cleaner above the baker's shop in Edgware, taking Terry with her every time.

My friend Janet Dixon who lived three doors away was an only child; her mother still carried her down stairs and dressed her every morning even though she was six years old and went to school. Her father was never out of work and Janet told me he worked in a factory making leather cases and handbags. I wished my father had a job like that!

My parents no longer smiled or laughed much and neither did Winnie and Arthur. Every day when I came out of school all the mothers looked sad and I kept hearing the words 'Hitler' and 'War'. Because television was in its infancy and only transmitted to a very few people, and news on the wireless was brief, children of my age were happily ignorant of what war meant.

Then, one day that summer, the British Government issued everyone with a gas mask contained in a strong cardboard box with a stout string shoulder strap; school premises were used for their distribution and our little family joined a long queue in a local school yard and there was a lot of talk about soldiers going to war; we were shown how to wear our gas masks and told to carry them at all times in case of a gas attack. I found they had a very unpleasant smell.

Wherever we went we began to see young men wearing the uniforms of soldiers, sailors and airmen. Like us they all carried their gas masks and something which I discovered was called a kit bag, full of their gear. I saw large sacks which turned out to be sandbags outside the large Co-operative Department store in Burnt Oak and in front of the factories along the main road to Colindale; and strange objects looking like enormous grey balloons with ears. appeared in the sky above the De Havilland aircraft factory. My Dad told me they were called 'barrage balloons' and were there to prevent enemy aircraft getting near enough to drop bombs and the sand bags were there to protect buildings and people from bomb blast. Consequently I began to have nightmares which I can still remember, about bomber planes and German soldiers marching up the alley way behind our house and getting through our French window to take my father away to prison. I would wake up screaming and crying. Consequently my parents' sleep began to be disturbed as well, so much so that I heard my Dad tell my Mum in desperation, 'Give her a good slap...' Years later I chided him about it. My mother I'm glad to say did not smack me.

One evening an Air Raid Warden called at our house wearing a tin hat and gave my parents instructions on how to protect our windows from bomb blast by putting sticky tape strips across the window panes. He told my Mum that she had to buy blackout material to make curtains for the windows to hide the electric lights and that it would be an offence to show even a chink of light which might help the German bomber planes. I heard him say that the street lights would soon be switched off and a torch would be needed if we went out after dark and that petrol rationing for the few cars in existence then was about to begin, which would affect uncle Arthur. The Warden told my Dad that he had been taught how to set off a siren when enemy aircraft were seen in the sky, followed by an All Clear siren when they had departed.

For weeks our parents must have been talking about the prospect of war and done a lot of heart searching. Winnie and Arthur came to see us the next day and as they left they gave us special hugs and kisses, and Mummy and Winnie cried. I had never seen them do that. Then my parents told us that because of the War we were going to stay in Wales for a little while, taking with us my friend Janet Dixon.

Just two days before the Second World War began the street lamps in Edgware were turned off and car head lights were blacked out. Buses and trains were fitted with dim blue lights and air raid wardens were permitted to reprimand people when house lights showed after dark.

We got up very early on the morning of Sunday 3rd September 1939 and one of our neighbours who owned a small car drove us to Paddington Great Western Railway station together with Janet and her parents: we children were being removed from the possible danger of imminent war. I was seven, Terry was almost five and Janet was six years old.

That morning Paddington station with its spectacular glass roof supported by iron girders was extremely crowded. Every platform was full of people boarding trains with many carriages, pushed by enormous steam locomotives belching black smoke and smuts of coal from their funnels. When each train was full of passengers and all the doors were shut a guard blew a whistle and waved a green flag which was the signal for the engine driver to move the train, which made a tremendous noise and blew a loud whistle as it did so. We held our mothers' hands tightly while our fathers, carrying our luggage, pushed their way through the crowds before us and found the train to take us to South Wales. They clambered aboard, found us seats and deposited our cases in the luggage rack above our heads before kissing us goodbye. We left them standing forlornly on the station platform surrounded by people waiting either to board another train out of London, or to say a tearful goodbye to those who did. Then as the train began to move we settled down in the crowded carriage. Later that morning after we left London my father eventually made his way to uncle Will and auntie Beat at the Evans Hotel in Euston and as he did so an air raid warning sounded and he and other people rushed to air raid shelters carrying their gas masks.

Until the 'Crisis' was over we three children were on our way to the little town of Burry Port, Carmarthenshire, in south Wales to stay with my mother's eldest sister Lizzie and her husband Jim Ogborn.

A WELSH CHILDHOOD

CHAPTER SIX

School Days in Wales

On that momentous day in 1939 when so many people left London because of the threat of war our journey by steam train to Wales was truly memorable. The train had many carriages and in each compartment every seat was taken and those passengers who had no seat had to stand or sit on their luggage in the corridors; there was an intense feeling of fear and apprehension with everyone carrying a gas mask. It took a long time to reach our destination: the public toilet on the train was difficult to reach with so much luggage and passengers in the way, and was supposed to be used only when the train was in motion. This was a problem when the engine driver was forced to stop many times in the middle of nowhere and my mother explained the train stopped because the signal was against us.

We had no idea how long our journey would take and gradually became used to the huffing, puffing and whistling of the steam engine and the rhythmic sound as it ran along the rails. We stopped at one or two stations when yet more people tried to board and after what seemed a long time we heard an extra loud and long whistle from the engine which made us jump in fright and immediately someone in our compartment got up and closed the windows, and the carriage lights came on

My mother had made the journey several times and she told us that that particular whistle was the engine driver's way of letting us know that our train about to go through a long dark tunnel under the river Severn which would take several minutes. Frightened by the noise in the tunnel even with the windows shut we huddled close to our mothers until it was over. Four miles in length, it was the longest in the British Isles when it was opened in 1879: it is still in use in the twenty first century, a hundred and twenty five years later.

The first stop in Wales was at Newport, and as we pulled into the station there, the platforms to and from London were packed with people and I saw many men in army uniform carrying kit bags with faces set like stone: some women were crying and one fell down and lay still; everyone carried a gas mask. The atmosphere in our carriage was tense as my mother stood up and opened the window and leaned out to ask what was happening. There was a deadly silence in our compartment when I heard a voice say 'Our Prime Minister had just announced on the wireless "We are at war with Germany." '

As we continued on our journey further into Wales passengers began to disembark. We saw many coal trucks and our train passed close by the enormous steel works in Port Talbot. Finally, after running through fields and open countryside, we arrived at Burry Port station tired and dishevelled. My mother went along to thank the engine driver for a safe journey, and then carrying our luggage and gas masks we left Station Road and walked through fields up an old tramway that had been used in the nineteenth century to ferry coal to the railway from an open cast mine at the back of the town. We reached the gate of a former level crossing which let us out on to Colby Road and just as we children were beginning to wonder how much further we would have to walk, particularly

Uncle Jim Ogborn on balcony of Rhandir Delyn.

Terry with his little legs, we passed a row of terraced cottages and stopped just beyond them at the bottom of a narrow rutted country lane called Cwm Ifor Road. On one side of the lane was an old ivy clad wall and on the other a little stream with a high hedge. My mother said 'Look up there. That's auntie Lizzie's house!' On the hillside above we could see a detached redbrick house with a large garden sloping down in front and behind it many trees topped with lots of birds nests.

We made our way up the stony lane to a large wooden gate which my mother pushed open, and we climbed up a path with banks on either side which gave off a strong scent of roses and the sound of buzzing bees, finally reaching steps which led to a balcony where Lizzie and Jim were standing at their open front door.

Their three bedroom detached house called 'Rhandir Delyn' was built in 1920. On the balcony were two small pillars with steps between them leading down into the front garden full of flowers and vegetables and on a low wall on either side of the pillars were highly perfumed rambling roses. At the side of the house was an orchard and another large garden.

Auntie Lizzie was forty three years old and a widow when she married Jim. They had been married for fourteen years. Her first husband had died of tuberculosis about twenty years before and she never had any children of her own. But being the eldest of a large family she was a little mother to all her brothers and sisters so she was accustomed to children of all ages. That is why she was prepared to take us on. She was small of stature, just five feet tall, bespectacled, rosy cheeked, grey haired and warm hearted and spoke with a soft Welsh accent. She was given to saying 'Oh dear!' frequently. Now, I too, am inclined to say it ! In her twenties she had been seriously ill and had had a kidney removed.

Jim, aged 40 years, was slightly built, five feet seven inches tall, olive complexioned, sporting a small black moustache with dark brylcreemed hair parted on one side. He had no accent and as a young man he had enjoyed swimming, cricket and football, at which he damaged a knee ligament and as a result he was not physically strong. They both loved working in their large garden and orchard, in which they grew a large variety of flowers, fruit and vegetables.

It must have been a daunting task that day for them to take on the responsibility of three little children they scarcely knew, between the ages of four and seven years - all of us about the age one of my little granddaughters is as I write down these memories.

We were all made very welcome by our aunt and uncle and astonishingly two days later Terry and I, and Janet too, cheerfully said good bye to our mothers. I heard my mother say as she departed, 'Don't worry Lizzie, everything will be back to normal by Christmas.'

WARTIME HOME

Our new 'home' was very different from that to which we had been accustomed We discovered the large birds nests in the woods behind the house were full of rooks, extremely noisy birds especially at dawn when they fly out to the fields to feed and at dusk when they return. The house was full of old fashioned furniture which did not match, some dark painted walls and sash windows. There was no electricity, no gas and no hot water or sanitation. In spite of this, Lizzie's home was spotless even though she did everything by hand.

We three children shared a bedroom at the front of the house, with two large sash windows and every night we said our prayers. Janet and I slept in an enormous four poster with metal knobs, under a colourful patchwork quilt, and Terry slept in a little single bed with his beloved golly. There was a chamber pot in a corner cupboard, and a marble topped table with a china basin, jug and soap dish, all beautifully decorated with painted flowers, stood between the windows with towels hanging on a rail beside it. Every morning auntie Lizzie took the jug and filled it with hot water for us to wash ourselves before getting dressed and going down to breakfast. As autumn progressed Lizzie lit a candle and carried it up the stairs to light our way to bed and placed it on our bedside table. Being the eldest it soon became my responsibility to blow out the candle when we had all settled down for the night, I learnt to be careful not to burn myself or spill candle wax.

The living room was dominated by an old fashioned fire place which had a cooking range with a black oven heated by coal where Lizzie baked bread every week. Either side of it were wall cupboards and old easy chairs with large cushions and wooden arms. Every day, except in high summer, Lizzie rose early to black lead the range before lighting the fire on which a kettle was usually singing as we came down to breakfast. Above the fireplace on either end of a very high mantelpiece stood two candle sticks and several ornaments: there was one of the Three Brass Monkeys, 'Hear No Evil, See No Evil, Speak No Evil'; there were charity boxes and a couple of religious texts. I recall one which said:

'Christ is the Head of this House,
An Unseen Guest at every Meal
A Silent Listener to every Conversation'.

The clothes airer hanging from the mantle piece, the coal scuttle, tongs and fender, were all made of brass and attached to each corner of the fender were leather topped box seats, one for newspaper and one for kindling wood. We discovered these seats were great places on which to sit and get warm when we came home from school on a winter's day.

Permanently standing in the centre of the room in the middle of the dining table surrounded by chairs was an oil lamp with a large white shade which Jim lit every evening at dusk. At meal times when Lizzie laid beautifully embroidered table cloths it was carefully lifted and gently replaced. As it was the only light in the room after dark we learnt to treat it with great respect, and we never ran about in the house. Lizzie said grace before meals and taught us to thank God before leaving the table. We were always encouraged to clear our plates. Lizzie would say 'Eat up, there are thousands starving in China!' and 'Don't leave the crusts, they will make your hair curl!'

On the wall, above a sideboard laden with pewter, a large framed print of the Laughing Cavalier by Frans Hals looked down on us and at first we felt his eyes followed us wherever we went in the room. Under the window was a treadle sewing machine and work basket and a small bed settee used by visitors and near the kitchen door hung a wall mirror, hair brush and a pipe stand: uncle Jim enjoyed an occasional pipe of tobacco. A small chiming pendulum clock, always fifteen minutes fast, hung near the hall doorway; Jim liked it that way!

The rather primitive kitchen at the back of the house under the bank of trees, where Lizzie cooked our food on a small oil stove, was lit by candles after dark and on gloomy days. Under the win-

Terry aged five.

dow stood a stone sink and cold water tap where Lizzie did all her washing by hand, except for bed linen which she sent to a laundry. Facing the sash window was a large Welsh dresser laden with dishes, jugs and commemorative mugs. Now I collect them, for they remind me of my childhood.

There was a bath at one end of the kitchen which was filled twice a week with buckets of water heated on the oil stove; for Lizzie and Jim on Friday night and for us children on Saturday night: Terry being the dirtiest was always last in. Due to government wartime regulations only five inches of bath water was allowed! During the second world war there was a very well known brand of shampoo called Amami, advertised on hoardings which said 'Friday Night is Amami night'. Most people customarily washed their hair once a week, usually on a Friday night, which became known as Amami night. We always had our hair washed then to make sure we had clean hair for church on Sundays.

Adjoining the kitchen, beside the cupboard under the stairs, was a long dark pantry lit by a very small window, full of wonderful aromas with three long shelves holding jars of bottled fruit, pickles and jam preserves, and at waist level was a sizeable marble shelf for cold food, vital before fridges. When we had birthday parties the pantry and the cupboard under the stairs directly opposite the wooden back door of the house, with bolts top and bottom, were ideal places for playing hide and seek on wet days.

The ground floor with the exception of the front room was covered with red stone tiles and attractive rag rugs, which Lizzie made, sitting with her back to the dining room window to catch the last of the day light before Jim lit the oil lamp. Every week she lifted the rugs,draped them over the washing line behind the house and struck them with a carpet beater before getting down on her knees to wash the stone floors with a bucket of hot water, a large scrubbing brush and a block of Fairy soap; as I grew older I got down on my knees to scrub the tiles in the entrance hall.

Lizzie and Jim's front room was modern by comparison: it had patterned wall paper, a wooden floor and a carpet. The modern fire place with a companion set and coal scuttle and easy chairs on either side was lit on wintry weekends; an ornate clock and a dainty oil lamp stood on the mantelpiece and in one corner of the room there was a cupboard full of games, and a large glass cabinet contained precious china and many books. In the centre of the room was a gate leg table, a wireless running on accumulator batteries stood on a cupboard at the sash window through which it was earthed. The batteries were heavy, made of metal and glass, full of liquid with a metal handle: eventually it became my responsibility to take these batteries to be recharged every few weeks.

The most unusual feature of their 'front room' was an organ on which stood two large candle sticks and a music stand and what intrigued us most about the organ were the stops and pedals. We were delighted when uncle Jim sat down on the music stool and demonstrated how they worked, by playing tunes for us from a music book called 'Songs to Remember'.

The greatest difference for us three little children, rudely uprooted from London suburbia on the day War was declared, was Lizzie and Jim's outside loo; it was in a little shed, behind and slightly to one side of the house, across the back yard under the bank of woodland: inside this little shed was a hinged wooden seat with a hole in the middle, and under the hole stood a large bucket. The 'toilet paper' was an old copy of Radio Times cut into

My London friend Janet Dixon with Lizzie and Jim at Rhandir Delyn.

four, threaded on a string and hung on a nail attached to the white washed wall. Inside this shed were lots of spiders and wood lice! If the ill fitting door was open there was an excellent view of and for any visitors to the house. I can still recall the smell of this privy, and see my little brother Terry happily sitting there with the door wide open singing at the top of his voice and kicking his heels against the wooden seat: also, after a few weeks I realised what it was that uncle Jim buried in the garden every week: the soil, extremely fertile, produced great vegetables the following year, especially potatoes! In 2002 I heard it said that Queen Victoria used newspaper for the toilets in Balmoral castle: I wonder if her vegetable garden was as fertile!

A WELSH CHILDHOOD

CHAPTER SEVEN

Church and School

Looking back to my childhood, Wales seemed to be a very reli-gious country. On Sundays everyone wore their best clothes, entertainment and sport were frowned upon and public houses and cinemas were shut (although I think an occasional workmen's club was open). I had the impression that most people went to chapel or church at least once every Sunday. People who attended Chapel were Welsh speaking and Lizzie and Jim's parish church of St Mary's held two Sunday morning services, one in Welsh, fol-lowed by one in English at which the congregation was much larg-er. It was a tradition that all females covered their heads in church or chapel. In 1942 the Archbishop of Canterbury, William Temple, decreed that because it was wartime this custom was no longer necessary. As a young woman Lizzie had been a Methodist like her father, but now both she and Jim were members of the Church in Wales and pillars of the local parish church of St Mary, attending an English speaking service there twice every Sunday.

After morning service on that first Sunday we met many of the congregation. They made a big fuss of us three little children 'down from London.' We heard them speaking in English with a Welsh accent about the War and children called 'Evacuees' who were coming from London to stay with local families. A few days later we saw the evacuees coming out of the railway station, carrying a few belongings and gas masks and wearing labels with their names

107

on attached to their coats. When we saw their anxious faces, we felt lucky because we were staying with Lizzie and Jim, and so did Janet.

We started school together in a day or two and Lizzie took us for the first week. After that we found our way there and back, getting lost only once. Janet and I were in separate classes of twenty four pupils in the Junior Girls' school and Terry was in the Infants next door. He had his fifth birthday at the end of September. The teachers and local children were extremely kind to us. Fortunately there was no uniform, although Terry like all school boys wore a cap and short grey trousers. One day we discovered a sweet shop in the front room of a house near the tramway in Colby Road. It had shelves lined with large jars of boiled sweets and a counter with a weighing scale. We often stopped there on the way to school and bought a halfpenny worth of sweets in a paper poke. We all loved pear drops and mint humbugs and sometimes bought a packet of sherbet with a liquorice stick straw.

At first we carried our gas masks all the time and wore them for a few minutes in class every day. I hated mine. It had an obnoxious smell. Our schoolroom windows all had crossed strips of sticky tape in case of bomb blast, which we never experienced in Burry Port. Once we had adjusted to the Welsh accent we settled down and made friends easily. I sat at a single desk with an ink well (a little pot fitted into a hole in the desk), a pen with a nib, an exercise book and lots of blotting paper, just in case we spilt the ink. The teacher used white chalk on a blackboard on the wall at the front of the class, behind her desk. In a few weeks I became ink monitor, responsible for refilling ink wells in my class.

I learnt my mathematical tables up to twelve times twelve, by rote, and I can still remember them. At morning playtime we each had a small bottle of milk to drink with a straw and we took sandwiches to school for dinner time. Twenty five years later our son Malcolm was also given a bottle of milk at school every morning until the Education Minister, Margaret Thatcher, in the Heath Conservative Government, put a stop to it, except for the very young.

We were the first evacuees at the school and every one made us welcome. Most of those who arrived a week later to stay with strangers were several years older than we were so we had little to do with them. Janet and I learnt the words of the Welsh song 'Dafydd yr Garreg Wen' which we sang together in Welsh at morning assembly one morning and received a round of applause! At going home time, our class always sang the hymn 'Now the Day is Over'. Afterwards I met Janet and Terry in the playground and we played games with school friends all the way back to Rhandir Delyn, arriving with a healthy appetite in time for tea. We never really felt the effect of food rationing because of Lizzie and Jim's large garden full of fruit and vegetables and the farms round about which supplied eggs on the 'Black Market'. Shop bread did become very grey in colour as the war progressed and we occasionally had to eat it, but it was not rationed until after the War.

SUNDAYS

Lizzie told us that children did not play outside on Sundays even in the summertime. But as long as we had clean hands, she allowed us to play quietly in the front room with jigsaws and playing cards and look at the many books in the cabinet. There were Treasure Island, Robinson Crusoe and all the Dickens novels; as I grew older

I thoroughly enjoyed reading them and we all liked looking at a large album of old postcards which today would be a collectors' item. We often looked at several illustrated volumes of the first world war, known as The Great War. An abiding memory for me is the photograph in one of them of the famous nurse Edith Cavell, blindfolded and lying shot dead at the foot of a tree for assisting allied troops to escape from Belgium, with a large Prussian officer in a piked helmet standing over her with a gun in his hand. Years later I discovered a statue commemorating her in central London. In the book case there were also several large volumes of famous paintings, and picture books about the Royal Family, for Lizzie and Jim were royalists; and occasionally at weekends we were allowed to play records on a wind up gramophone.

For the next few years we went to church with them every Sunday and they drummed into us that the Bible said "Remember the sabbath day to keep it holy' and 'Six days shalt thou labour, and do all thy work: but the seventh day is the sabbath of the LORD thy God: thou shalt not do any work......' Lizzie did none except cook a roast dinner and a fruit pie after morning service. In the afternoon we three children attended Sunday school, and in the evening after tea we all went to the evening service. As a result I can honestly say that I know the book of Common Prayer and many Ancient and Modern hymns by heart. Although Terry and I had been baptised in the Catholic church my father raised no objections.

Just occasionally instead of going to church we stayed home on Sundays to listen to Morning Service on the wireless. Sometimes the preacher was the Reverend George Macleod speaking from the holy island of Iona. We all liked listening to his sermons. He was a very charismatic preacher.

BURRY ESTUARY

Rhandir Delyn was over a mile from the seashore and from a vantage point in the garden we could see little pilot ships guiding merchant vessels up and down the Burry estuary to and from Swansea Docks which was a major port then, carrying coal and weapons of war together with troop convoys. Swansea was also an important industrial centre for the manufacture of steel, tinplate, copper and aluminium. At sunset on a fine day the view across the estuary to Worms Head was quite spectacular and on moonlit nights uncle Jim sometimes stood with us to admire the view and he would pretend to be Scottish and say 'It's a braw bricht moonlicht nicht the nicht!' Only recently I discovered the reason why he did not have a Welsh accent - he was an Englishman!

Across the lane from our bedroom window, we could see a rather grand cream coloured Victorian mansion called Plas Newydd, with a tall monkey puzzle in its front garden. The house was built by Josiah Mason about 1860 and occupied for twenty five years by Howard Elkington of Warwick and his wife Anne. In the mid 1880s they moved to Mold and when he died his body was brought back and buried in nearby Pembrey Church. Elkington Road in Burry Port is named after him. From the mid 1880s Thomas Chivers from Maesteg in Glamorgan and his French wife and family owned Plas Newydd. He died in 1901 and we discovered that the entrance to Plas Newydd, at the junction of Colby Road and Church Hill, was called Chivers Corner. There we could catch a bus to the market town of Llanelly. But I have no idea who lived at Plas Newydd when we lived in Burry Port. As the dark nights drew in, we children discovered that the ivy on the old stone wall in Cwm Ifor Road, which separated us from the mansion, hid the nests of many bats, but that's another story.

THE WIRELESS

On Saturday afternoons Jim sat on a tapestry carver chair beside the wireless in the front room listening to football matches and the results. In those days football, either amateur or professional, was never played on a Sunday in Great Britain. Jim's favourite football player was Tom Finney, described by many as the best British footballer. He is still alive at the turn of the 21st century and Bill Shankley, the manager of Liverpool Football Club for many years, once said 'Tom Finney would have been great in any team, in any match, and in any age, even if he was wearing an overcoat!'

There were only two channels to listen to on the wireless during the war, the Home Service and the Light Programme. One day I was with uncle Jim when he was tuning in for the news on the Home Service and by chance he picked up a broadcast in English, from Germany. We heard the words 'Germany calling, Germany calling.' For a minute or two we listened together, transfixed, it was such a surprise. Afterwards uncle Jim told me that the speaker was William Joyce, known as 'Lord Haw Haw', and that it was really against the law to listen to him, because he said bad things about the British, telling us that Germany would win the war. 'But,' uncle Jim assured me, 'we will win the War.' I subsequently discovered that William Joyce lived in England in the nineteen twenties and was a fascist. He fled to Germany just before the Second World War and became an enemy agent. His broadcasts were full of propaganda and very anti British. At the end of the Second World War he was captured and tried in a British court of law because, although he was an Irish American, he had a British passport and an English mother and had been educated and lived in England most of his life. The trial lasted three days in September 1945 and he was found guilty of treason and the judge sentenced him to death by hanging. It went to the Court of Appeal, and the House of Lords upheld the sentence and he was hanged at Wandsworth prison early in 1946.

When we listened to the news on the BBC, the newscasters, John Snagg, Bruce Belfridge and Alva Liddell, always began by announcing their name so that people could recognise their voice, and accept their statements were genuine. Children's Hour, broadcast at five o'clock on weekdays, was introduced by Derek McCulloch, known as Uncle Mac. At the end of every programme he always said 'Good night children, everywhere.' Two of my favourite programmes were 'Toy Town' and 'The Biblical story of King David', after which I began to take an interest in the history of the world.

Every morning including Sundays a young milkman with horse and cart carrying a churn of fresh milk from the farm a mile up Cwm Ifor Road arrived at Lizzie's front door. She greeted him with a large jug taken from her Welsh dresser, into which he ladled two pints. She immediately stood the jug of milk in boiling water on the oil stove, scalding it to bring it to near boiling point. Then the cream rose to the top of the jug and prevented it from turning sour. The following morning we children were given the delicious cream on our porridge or cereal, followed by dried egg, a wartime product, made into an omelette; then just before we departed for school we ate a tablespoonful of cod liver oil and malt and some concentrated orange juice supplied by the State for children, because we had no oranges in this country during the second world war.

In a few weeks Lizzie arranged for Janet and me to have velour hats to wear for church on Sundays. Janet's was royal blue and mine was brown, to match our eyes, and I adored mine; I have liked hats ever since but motor cars tend to discourage their use and generally they only come into their own on special occasions. However, in this twenty first century global warming is a problem and so sun hats have become fashionable in a variety of shapes and colours and act as a protection in strong sunlight and I am delighted to see that our granddaughter likes wearing them.

Christmas 1939

During the Christmas holiday auntie Lizzie took us to Llanelly to see Father Christmas and our two mothers came down by train from London to spend the festive season with us. It was a joyful time. Mummy looked slim and pretty and it was wonderful to feel her arms around me. I cannot recall our father's presence. Father Christmas came in the night and left a pillowcase with toys and games for us. Terry had a train set, I had a sweet shop and Janet had a doll. After dinner on Christmas Day we all congregated in the front room to listen to King George speaking on the wireless to all the people of Great Britain and the British Empire. He quoted a poem which began 'I said to the man who stood at the gate of the year'. I liked it a lot and have enjoyed listening to and reading poetry ever since: many years later when I was on holiday in Scotland with our son Malcolm we were touring Stirling castle with a guide, who was an old soldier. He began to quote this poem spoken by King George, but his memory failed and to his delight I finished it.

In the New Year of 1940, our mothers returned to Edgware hop-

ing the war would soon be over, and auntie Lizzie told me who
Father Christmas really was and I kept it a secret!

CHAPTER EIGHT

War Time

In January 1940 the whole nation was issued with Identity cards and I can still remember my number! These cards had to be produced from time to time and although after the second world war they were no longer required, when the National Health Service began in 1948 those identity numbers became our individual National Health numbers for the next thirty years. Also that month every one in Great Britain was issued with a ration book containing a fixed amount of coupons for certain foods for every week of the year. If we wanted more we had to wait until the following week; meat rationing was introduced a few months later.

Recently I discovered an old ration book at a boot sale. I was so amazed to find the amount of food we were allowed each week during the second world war that I wrote it down: 2 eggs, 4 ozs fat, 2 ozs tea, 12 ozs sugar, 4 ozs cheese, 4 ozs jam and 4 ozs of bacon. Everyone had 'points' in the ration book for tinned foods and we were allowed three pints of milk a week. Meat was rationed too, but bread was not rationed until after the war. We were spared sweet rationing until 1942, then we were all allowed 3 ozs a week.

In late February my mother's youngest sister Mary married Jim Marcroft, an Englishman, in the parish church at Tunbridge Wells in Kent. They were both in the army. Mary was in the ATS and Jim was a chef in the Army Catering Corps. Because of the war my mother was the only member of our family present. Mary and Jim spent their honeymoon at our home in Edgware, and our parents made them as welcome as possible under the circumstances.

At Rhandir Delyn the Daily Herald was delivered every week day and Reynolds News on Sundays. Lizzie arranged for us to have the Dandy and Beano comics and the Children's Newspaper. After a while I was allowed to collect Enid Blyton magazines from the newsagent by the railway station.

Lizzie had a sewing machine and was an excellent seamstress and taught Janet and me how to embroider cushion covers, pillow cases and table cloths and make woolly pom-poms. We spent hours making raffia mats and doing French knitting with wool and a cotton reel with four nails in the top. We made teapot stands and kettle holders for our mothers and my many aunts. Uncle Jim produced a Meccanno set for Terry to play with and Janet and I sometimes helped him to construct a crane! When he grew up Terry became a carpenter and a construction engineer.

One night when I had just blown out the candle before we went to sleep we heard a strange clicking noise accompanied by an occasional squeak and were aware that something was flying about in our bedroom. Unknown to us several bats, attracted by the candle light through chinks in the curtains at our open sash windows, had entered the room and they were flying about in the dark trying to find their way out. We were very frightened and lay screaming under our blankets until auntie Lizzie came to our rescue and threw back the curtains and opened the windows wide to let them out. It happened on more than one occasion, sometimes even after we had fallen asleep without realising they were in our bedroom. Then we would be woken up by them and start shrieking for Lizzie. She would come to our rescue in a voluminous night gown, speaking in a strange voice because she'd left all her teeth in a pot beside her bed. I hate bats. I was under the mistaken impression that they would get tangled in my thick curly hair. One day that winter my hair needed cutting and Lizzie took me to the local barber, who cut off my curls. Sadly, they never grew back again.

In Great Britain during the whole of Lent no flowers adorn church altars and on Good Fridays throughout the second world war and for some years afterwards the wireless, and later television, broadcast nothing but religious programmes, classical music and the latest news. On that day only the bakers shops were open for the sale of Hot Cross Buns, which were never made or sold on any other day of the year. Then on the Saturday before Easter Sunday St Mary's, like most parish churches in Great Britain, was a hive of activity with flowers picked from the gardens of the congregation, including Lizzie's. We children helped decorate every nook and cranny of the church.

On Easter Day Janet and I went to church wearing straw bonnets and our mother sent Terry and me cardboard eggs full of chocolate buttons, with a toy motor car for him, and a little red ball for me, for my eighth birthday that month. Lizzie and Jim gave us all a special edition of the book 'The Life of Our Lord' written expressly for his own children by Charles Dickens. I still have this book but when Terry was in his teens he threw his away, and now regrets doing so. Auntie Lizzie would be proud of him because unlike me, he and his wife Joan are regular churchgoers.

Terry had outgrown the little bed he slept in so Lizzie moved him to the back bedroom where he had his own wash stand, a bowl and jug, and a large colour reproduction painting on the wall of 'Bubbles' by John Millais, which I have recently discovered was a

Nanny Maloney in old age.

wedding present given to auntie Lizzie when she married her first husband; in the bookcase downstairs was a Pears Cyclopaedia with a small copy of this painting just inside its front cover. The original purchaser of 'Bubbles' sold the painting to a man called Thomas J Barratt who was the son in law of Andrew Pears, the originator of Pears Soap; the artist, John Millais, gave his permission for the painting (of his own grandson) to be used to advertise Pears soap and its use as an illustration in Pears Cyclopaedia. But when I was a little girl Pears soap brought me out in a rash!

Of course our aunt and uncle had the biggest bedroom in Rhandir Delyn, with an enormous Bible lying on the top of their tallboy, a chamber pot, essential in every home without a water closet, and an oil lamp on their bedside table.

After church on Sunday evenings we occasionally went for sedate walks with them. Lizzie always wore a hat and on cool evenings she wore a fox fur round her neck which was highly fashionable in those days. A dead animal - ugh! Jim always looked very dapper carrying an elegant walking stick which he swung as he doffed his trilby hat to all the ladies we passed. But on wet Sunday evenings after church we sat in the front room while he played the organ instead. His favourite tune was 'Drink To Me Only With Thine Eyes'.

We made friends with the Welsh speaking children who lived in The Terrace at the foot of Cwm Ifor Road. Their homes were small, just two up and two down with an open range fire, a scullery and privies in little wooden shacks half way up their back gardens, but unlike Rhandir Delyn their homes all had electric lights. Janet made no attempt to speak Welsh but Terry and I did, which amused Lizzie. She understood it but did not often speak the language. Terry's best friend was John Edwards whose father owned the farm in Colby Road. He and his wife spoke Welsh most of the time.

SPRINGTIME IN THE VALLEYS

Jim worked as a clerk on the Great Western Railway in Llanelly, three miles from Burry Port. He cycled there and back on a 'Rudge Whitworth' bike which he had to push up and down Cwm Ifor Road. His job entitled him and Lizzie to free rail travel and as they were now in loco parentis, we children were allowed to travel with them at a very cheap rate. From the Easter holidays in 1940 Lizzie took us on day trips to her childhood home in Cymmer. We loved these journeys on steam trains going up the south Wales mining valleys. It was such fun. We caught an 8am train from Burry Port which was always on time and as we went through Llanelly we would be on our feet to see Jim who always stood outside his railway office to wave to us. We were careful not to stick our heads out of the carriage window too often, for fear of smuts from the engine getting in our eyes or dirtying our clothes. We passed many goods trains laden with coal which, in those days, the whole of Great Britain depended upon. All railway stations had a goods yard where coal was deposited for merchants to bag and distribute by horse and cart to every house in the land for everyone had coal fires. Shop goods too were delivered in the same way.

We changed trains at Swansea to go up the Welsh valleys and even in the rain we got excited at the sight of the coal tips and the bare mountains with sheep dotted on them, and as we walked through the streets of Cymmer with the smell of coal hanging in the air we could hear sheep bleating on the mountainside and we would pass some of them in the street. Lizzie always stopped to talk to nursing mothers along the way and I was fascinated at the Welsh way they held their babies, wrapped in a huge shawl which was then wrapped around themselves leaving one hand free.

At 21 Lloyds Terrace, on the side of a mountain, my mother and all her brothers and sisters were born. There we found fun-loving Bessie and our little cousins Betty, Keith and baby Gillian. It was Gran Hill's home but she was away living in Margate. Opposite number 21 was a bare mountain where we could actually see and hear the sheep and little lambs and at the peak was a farmhouse ruin. A tributary of the river Afan flowed at the foot of this mountain and beside it ran a single track railway line between Cymmer and Abergwynfi, where our mother's sister Emily lived.

Gran Hill's house had five rooms with sash windows and a kitchen-scullery. To enter the front door we had to climb up several large stone steps from the street. All the houses in the terrace had coal bunkers under the front garden, a legacy from the time when miners lived in them and were entitled to free coal. The downstairs parlour had a fire place, a couple of easy chairs and an organ once used to entertain the family. There was a bookcase containing a Bible and many children's books which were Sunday school prizes to my mother and her brothers and sisters. The main living room had a dresser and a large dining table and chairs and beside an open fire cooking range and high mantelpiece a large carver chair stood with its back to the window.

In the tiled yard outside the back door a tin bath hung on the wall and beside it was a small room with a toilet. All bathing took place in the tin bath in front of the coal fire in the living room; upstairs were three bedrooms.

A number of large stone steps had been cut into the mountainside to reach a hilly back garden where there was a well-used clothes line, because washing was, of course, either done by hand or in a gas boiler. At the top of the garden Bessie's husband, Ron, had several hens in a coop. A strong back gate kept out the sheep and they freely grazed beyond it on the bare mountainside.

If the weather was dry, we went out of the back gate to play on the mountain with our cousins, but if it was wet there was nothing I liked better than sitting in the parlour reading the books 'Little Women' and 'Uncle Tom's Cabin'.

More than once on our return journey to Burry Port when we got off the train I squashed my hand in the carriage door as it swung to. Then, walking up the tramway to Rhandir Delyn with navy blue fingers held in the air was an unforgettably painful experience.

A FAMILY FUNERAL

One day Lizzie took me away from school to go to the funeral of her father's brother Thomas John Thomas, known as Tom. He died in 1940 at the age of sixty one and by all accounts he was a tall, friendly farmer in the village of Wick in Glamorgan. It was he who called frequently on Gran Hill with a basket of eggs when my mother was growing up. I do not think I ever met him. That day all the houses in Glyncorrwg had their front curtains closed as a mark of respect and I was surrounded by many adults all wearing black. Great uncle Tom was buried in the churchyard there.

Fifty years later a Welshman on his way to Gatwick airport to pick up a friend knocked at our front door in Caterham. He told me his name was Ron Thomas and he had just found out we were cousins. It was hardly surprising since our family is large. David and I made him welcome with tea and cake, and after some discussion and getting out a chart of our family tree we discovered that great uncle Tom was his grandfather. Ron, two years my junior, had also been in the house in Glyncorrwg on the day of the funeral, but neither of us remembered seeing each other. When he returned to Bridgend we corresponded for a year until he died suddenly.

DUNKIRK AND WINSTON CHURCHILL

In May 1940 Winston Churchill became our Prime Minister and in the children's matinee at the cinema we saw him wearing a siren suit (like a quilted track suit), smoking a cigar and giving his famous victory sign with his fingers. He looked very old to me. One morning at the end of that month we heard the BBC newscaster say that many little ships and boats from England were going to France to pick up our soldiers who were trapped by the Germans on the beaches of Dunkirk in France. We heard stories of bravery on the BBC news and saw pictures of the evacuation in the newsreels at the cinema. For a few days there was a strange silence about the town of Burry Port. I could sense a feeling of deep anxiety everywhere and I heard people say with ashen faces that our island was standing alone.

Then we three children joined Lizzie and Jim in the front room at Rhandir Delyn to listen to Mr. Churchill on the wireless making what was to become a famous speech. I have heard it repeated many times since, and though I was only eight years old I still recall the hair standing up on the back of my neck when he said '......we shall defend our island, whatever the cost may be, we shall fight on the beaches, we shall fight on the landing grounds, we shall fight in the fields and in the streets, we shall fight in the hills; we shall never surrender.' Though I was very frightened it made me feel proud to be British. No one liked the Germans during the War.

HOME GUARD

A short while before all this happened uncle Jim Ogborn had joined the Home Guard, a platoon of male volunteers of the older generation whose job it was to protect the town from enemy attack; so, with an imminent threat of invasion by Germany, Jim's platoon was summoned to a meeting at the Gwendraeth hotel that night. They discussed what further measures they could take, and having already put up barbed wire defences along the seashore they decided to change and remove road signs in the country lanes of Carmarthenshire to confuse the enemy if they landed in Wales. Our government issued posters which uncle Jim helped paste on hoardings or shop windows in the town, with slogans, like 'Dig for Victory' to encourage people to grow their own vegetables, and 'Careless Talk Costs Lives'; and strangers were treated with deep suspicion, for a while.

A BRIEF HOLIDAY

Early that summer, despite the threat of invasion, Janet's parents Flo and Gilbert Dixon together with our Mum and Dad came to spend a short holiday with us. We showed them the way to Burry Port dock and the light house and we spent the afternoon on the sand dunes. Then we went on three coach trips: the first was round the Burry estuary to the picturesque Gower coast, culminating in Rhossili Bay which was absolutely breathtakingly beautiful that day; the second trip was to St David's in Pembrokeshire to see the cathedral built in his name, where we learnt he was the

Great Aunt Gwen when she was a young woman.

Patron Saint of Wales; the third trip was a day spent in the Brecon Beacons to visit some magical caves. To reach the caves we had to travel through the Welsh valleys and Flo was so frightened by the steep narrow curving roads that she persuaded the coach driver to let her get out and walk down the mountainsides, while we waited for her at the bottom. I became travel sick and was given a stick of barley sugar to suck, which helped! Before they returned to Edgware Janet's parents told us they slept in a Morrison shelter in their sitting room. It was a steel table with a double bed underneath. My parents could not afford a shelter. All too quickly the holiday was over and they returned to London and we went back to school.

One day Janet and I listened to Children's Hour on the wireless and when it was followed by the six o'clock news, auntie Lizzie and uncle Jim joined us and we all listened to the newscaster say that German aircraft were bombing London and other cities, day and night and it was called 'The Battle of Britain'. The newscasters paid tribute to our brave Spitfire and Hurricane pilots many of whom lost their lives in shooting down German bomber planes. Afterwards we heard Mr. Churchill speaking about the pilots, saying 'Never in the field of human conflict was so much owed by so many to so few.'

We saw the news in the children's matinee at the cinema on the Saturday afternoon and Janet and I cried together in bed that night. Lizzie and Jim comforted us as best they could. Fortunately, Terry was too young to understand. The battle went on all summer and reached a climax on 15th September 1940. When peace was restored years later, those of us who lived through the second world war remember those brave men especially on that date, and give grateful thanks for what they did.

ABERKENFIG

In the summer of 1940 Lizzie took us on the train to Aberkenfig to see Nanny Maloney. We walked from the station through the village to the little terrace house where she lived. It had just a kitchen and a living room with a curtain in the corner, hiding a little staircase leading to the bedrooms where my Dad, Winnie and Griff were born. Her water closet was just outside the back door. I thought Nanny looked very tiny, even smaller than Lizzie and her hair was whiter than ever. Griff was there and while Nanny and Lizzie drank tea, he took us wimberry picking in the fields nearby. It was great fun. Like the other wild fruits, dewberries and blackberries, they are delicious in a fruit pie or stewed with cream. Lizzie and Jim grew every imaginable fruit in their garden, except cherries, which made me sad because I loved them, and strawberries which I never tasted until long after the war.

Jim had a charming good looking cousin of about his own age who lived in Swansea. He and his wife were childless and often came to visit Lizzie and Jim. At first I enjoyed their visits because Jim's cousin made a great fuss of me in particular, and said nice things to me. He liked to draw me aside and talk to me on my own and one sunny day holding me by the hand he took me out into the garden through the orchard and began lifting me up into the trees and catching me when I jumped down. I did not like the way he ran his hands over me and kissed me and attempted to carry me, much as my father used to do at home when I was little. I was eight years old and thought myself far too grown up for that sort of behaviour and felt instinctively that something was wrong. I did not like him any more. In fact he frightened me and I ran back to the house. When he and his wife had departed I told auntie Lizzie.

I am glad to say they never ever came to the house again when I was there. Many years later I told my brother Terry about my experience and he said that he had never liked him either!

CHAPTER NINE

Living in Wales

Back home in Edgware Mum and Dad were having many sleepless nights. With no shelter of their own they refused to use the poorly ventilated brick street shelter and so they stayed in bed as many did during the air raids; they had little sleep and Mummy's health began to suffer. This period of the war was known as The London Blitz. One morning we heard on the wireless that the city of London and the docks lay in ruins but St Paul's cathedral remained standing and Lizzie said it was a miracle. At the same time the Germans were dropping bombs on many other British cities.

Prayers were said in church every Sunday and we said our prayers every night before bed. In the newsreels at the children's matinee we saw what happened when a siren went off, how the people in London ran to shelters in basements and underground stations. We watched newsreels about our soldiers, sailors and airmen including our brave Spitfire and Hurricane pilots defending our island Whenever the German Chancellor Adolf Hitler appeared on the cinema screen there was uproar and we all booed loudly. But we all cheered whenever Churchill appeared. on the screen. Terry Janet and I liked watching films of Laurel and Hardy, The Three Stooges or a Hopalong Cassidy cowboy film. In school holidays we played cowboys and Indians in the woods behind Rhandir Delyn making dens out of bracken and dashing for home if we saw a snake in the long grass!

We had long since ceased carrying our gas masks every where because I do not recall any air raids in Burry Port. But blackout restrictions were enforced and moonlit nights were magical the night sky was black velvet, with stars twinkling like hundreds of diamonds. More than once from Colby Road I saw a shooting star in the Milky Way. Now in the twenty first century we have so many street lights that we seldom see the night sky except during a power cut. Unknown to Terry and me, in the autumn of 1940 at the age of thirty three our father was conscripted into the army. Meanwhile my uncle Harry was in the Eighth Army and auntie Millie and my cousins John and Ivor together with our Gran Hill moved away from Margate on the Kent coast and went to live in the comparative safety of Staffordshire.

I particularly remember the day in the winter of 1940 when Lizzie cried because one night the city of Coventry was devastated by German bombers, five hundred people were killed and the cathedral was destroyed. The streets of Burry Port were silent when that news came through on the BBC and many prayers were said in church and chapels throughout Wales.

Shortly afterwards our Mum and Dad came down to see us. We were wild with excitement at the sight of them and amazed to see my father in army uniform. Mummy looked tired and I heard her telling Lizzie about the dreadful air raids, but her face was radiant whenever she looked at my father. She obviously adored him. Early one morning while it was still dark and cold she woke us because our Dad was leaving to report to an army depot. Locked in an embrace our parents said an emotional good bye at auntie Lizzie's open front door with Terry and me clinging to their legs crying. It was awful. To cheer us up for Christmas that year we were given an easel and blackboard, lots of coloured chalks, colouring books, crayons and plasticine. I remember singing carols in church and saying lots of prayers.

BOMBING OF SWANSEA

A few weeks after Christmas in February 1941 our sleep was disturbed by the distant sound of gunfire and exploding bombs. Terry slept through it but Janet and I trembled under our patch-work quilt: we were sure we were being invaded. In the morning we heard the news on the BBC that the Germans had bombed Swansea, 15 miles from Burry Port with the intention of destroying the docks there but they hit the town centre instead. Jim had left for work by the time we heard the news and at breakfast auntie Lizzie kept on worrying about his brother Trevor and the rest of Jim's family who lived there. After two more nights of the bombing of Swansea we heard the sad news that Jim's favourite aunt and uncle who lived there had gone to their shelter on one of those dreadful nights and it had received a direct hit, killing them outright, yet their house remained standing. We were all sad because they were a dear old couple whose garden backed onto the railway line and they often waved to us as our train passed by on the way to the Afan valley. On a subsequent train journey we saw the large crater in their garden. Consequently Janet's parents decided she would be just as safe at home in Edgware and her mother came to fetch her and I had to get used to sleeping on my own.

Wales celebrates its patron saint's day on the 1st March and if it fell on a school day we children had the afternoon off. Traditionally if it was not raining we and some of our school friends took a picnic and went up the lane past the farm and over stiles, exploring an old slate quarry then through the woods, ending up in the cemetery where we played hide and seek. Lizzie and Jim are now buried there. We always returned ravenously hungry. In those war time days of our childhood we were never accompanied by adults and the front door of Rhandir Delyn was seldom closed in daylight hours except in bad weather. Very occasionally tramps would appear at the door asking for a drink and Lizzie always made them welcome. Jim never lit the oil lamp until it was quite dark because Lizzie said 'We must make the most of God's light.'

That Easter holiday Lizzie took us to Swansea to see Jim's brother Trevor and his family: as we walked through the streets to his home in the Hafod the town centre lay in ruins while Swansea docks, the Germans' intended target, was still intact.

On the way to and from and at school I played wonderful rhyming games with my friends and we had crazes for playing with whipping tops or skipping ropes, and ball games, while Terry kicked a football with his friend John Edwards, or ran to school with an iron hoop and rod. His pockets often bulged with marbles or conkers depending on the season and sometimes I played with them too. Like all school boys he wore short grey trousers until the age of fourteen, when many boys left school. Only when they started working for a living did they wear long trousers.

A favourite girls' game was hopscotch which I played with my friends on the pavement in Colby Road, in school, or on the balcony at Rhandir Delyn. On warm sunny days we all loved playing hide and seek in Lizzie and Jim's garden for we could hide in the orchard and run all round the house; we collected caterpillars and grasshoppers among the apple trees and played with them on the garden steps.

On my ninth birthday Lizzie made some cakes and gave me a tea party. As it was a wet day my school friends and I played musical chairs, pass the parcel, blind man's buff, and put the tail on the donkey . At this age I became very friendly with Dilys Webb, an eleven year old Welsh girl from the Terrace in Colby Road.

LETTER WRITING

The only way to keep in touch with relatives and distant friends during the war was by writing letters using a pen with a nib and a bottle of ink or a fountain pen. Lizzie was a great correspondent and kept her brothers and sisters together in this way by writing to them all and passing on the latest family news. As a consequence the postman was a frequent visitor to Rhandir Delyn.

In the spring of 1941 her brother our uncle Bill was in the Royal Corps of Signals stationed in the west of England and about to leave for the Western Desert somewhere in Africa. He had a baby boy called Terry and his wife Kitty decided to go to see Bill for a few days before his embarkation, taking with her baby Terry and Dinda, their faithful springer spaniel, who was devoted to Bill. They spent a couple of days with him there and then Bill had to return to his barracks prior to departure the following day. Next morning Kitty, with Terry in a push chair and Dinda on a lead, was walking to the railway station to go back home when she heard the sound of marching feet. Dinda became very excited and broke free from his lead and Kitty with baby Terry chased after him, to find him running through the regiment of marching soldiers until he found Bill. The Commanding Officer was forced to order the troops to stop so that Kitty could retrieve Dinda and say goodbye to Bill.

During the War years there was a programme on the Wireless called 'Forces Requests' played by the concert organist Sandy McPherson, which was relayed to the troops wherever they were. Lizzie wrote a letter asking Sandy to play a tune for her brother Bill and we listened to him play it. I have a photo of my two uncles Bill and Harry, taken when they were in the Eighth Army in the Western Desert, and Mary's husband, Jim, who was serving in the Catering Corps told me years later that he met up with them when they were all fighting the Germans in Italy at the latter end of the War.

One day there was an explosion on the sea shore in Burry Port and when a member of the Home Guard went to investigate he was horrified to discover that children had crept under the barbed wire to play on the sands and one of them, an evacuee, was killed by a mine washed up with the tide. The whole town was deeply shocked.

We were all issued with enough clothing coupons for a year. Auntie Bessie and my mother were popular with friends and family because they were both good at making new out of old, Bessie with material and my Mum with wool. Because coupons were in short supply lisle stockings became popular for they lasted much longer than silk stockings. Nylons and tights had not been invented and all stockings had seams down the back of the leg. Some young women without coupons for stockings stained their legs with tea or gravy browning and then got someone to make a line down the back of their legs to look like a seam. In church one Sunday I heard that wedding dresses were being passed round a family to be worn again.

In the Whitsun holidays Lizzie took us to see our Nanny again, and afterwards we walked from her house in Aberkenfig to the top of Sarn Hill to see her sister, auntie Sue, a tall lady who wore her brown hair in a bun. She and her husband Len had four sons, my Dad's first cousins. She was a warm hearted lovely lady who liked children and that day she told us our aunt Winnie and little Ronald were coming to stay with her for the duration of the War. Auntie Sue had been a teacher before she married; in those days that profession did not employ married women and she became a housewife. Her husband uncle Len bred rabbits, and Terry and I were delighted to find several adorable little bunnies on their front lawn and we were allowed to play with them. Later we spent a riotous afternoon with their four extremely active sons. Kenneth, the youngest, was my age; he became a rugby player of some distinction when he grew up: in 1961 when our son Malcolm was a baby I saw Ken on TV playing for Wales in an international rugby match and I felt very proud. Years later he played rugby league at Salford, and in 1970 we read in the national press that he had been killed in a road accident. Auntie Sue, by then a widow, was simply devastated

A WELSH CHILDHOOD

CHAPTER TEN

Burry Port

Tucked away in the grounds of Rhandir Delyn beyond the orchard was a small wooden bungalow, where an elderly couple called Spillsbury lived with their daughter, and small grandson and a little dog. If Terry saw Mr Spillsbury going out in the evening with his dog he would ask him where he was going. He always got the same answer: 'To see a man about a dog!' which puzzled us until we discovered it meant he was going to the local public house though of course he never went there on a Sunday for they were closed. Terry and I taught his grandson Simon to walk and talk. Simon's mother was a milliner who used to alter hats to fit me. One day when he was four years old I took him to play in the woods behind Rhandir Delyn. We enjoyed ourselves until he bent down and picked up a snake. It was harmless, but we ran home! Years later I heard that although he was under age Simon enlisted in the army at the age of sixteen to escape the cramped conditions in that little bungalow.

One day a dentist visited our primary school and extracted one of my teeth in the head mistress' room and I longed for my mother. I needed a cuddle! It was the only time I saw a dentist until the National Health Service started when I was sixteen. Children did not suffer greatly from tooth decay during the second world war probably because the diet was good and we did not have many sweets. A pretty Gipsy girl with long red hair joined our class and infected us all with head lice, reminding me yet again how much I missed my mother who was now living alone in Edgware. She wrote to Lizzie to say she had taken a full time job and had two nurses as lodgers to help pay the mortgage, and keep her company at night.

I remember writing her two letters, one to say that Terry had become a choir boy at St Mary's church and that he wore brylcreem on his hair with what was known as a choir boy parting, and the other that I had become a Brownie, and loved my uniform dress, large yellow tie and brown wool beret: I told her that I had been taken to Llanelly by my Brown Owl to be presented with a prize by Lady Baden Powell; the Founder of the Brownies and Girl Guides, for growing the best daffodil in a pot. (They are the emblem of Wales.)

We Brownies had weekly meetings in the Memorial Hall near an obelisk commemorating Amelia Earhart who was the first woman to pilot a plane across the Atlantic in 1928, landing at Burry Port in a seaplane called 'Friendship'.

Auntie Winnie wrote to tell us she and little Ronald had arrived in Sarn to live with auntie Sue, and Lizzie took us to see them. We had a lovely day and on the way up Sarn Hill we met some German prisoners of war who were working on the roads and lived in a camp in Bridgend. Auntie Lizzie stopped to speak to them and their English was good.

NEW STREET

Uncle Tom Bowen was born in Burry Port and in his old age he told me that when he was young he and his brothers and sister went to the same primary school as we did, and like Terry he was a choir boy at St Mary's church and attended Sunday school. Uncle Jim, twelve years his senior, was his Sunday school teacher and Tom was very disruptive in class, for he liked fooling about and had the ability to tell the most wonderful tales, which were far more entertaining to the other children than listening to Jim Ogborn telling Bible stories. Time passed and Tom grew up. My mother's sister Addie was in service for a while working for a Mrs Mann who lived in the large house which has since been demolished, opposite St Mary's church. Addie met Tom at the church several times and one day after morning service, Lizzie and Jim invited them both to tea and they fell in love and of course they married in 1939 and Tom joined the Fleet Air Arm at the outbreak of second world war.

Tom's mother, a widow known to us as Granny Bowen, still lived in the family home in New Street in a terraced house with a front door just a step off the pavement at the bottom of Church Hill. Tom, his brothers and his sister Muriel were all born there and when Muriel got married she and her husband John Mexam continued to live with Granny Bowen. The narrow dark rooms of the house were lit by gas light and the parlour, seldom used, was kept just for special occasions. The main living room had a large old fashioned kitchen range and the tiny scullery contained only a gas cooker and a boiler for washing clothes, with a mains water tap just outside the back door next to an outside water closet. Because they had no sink, dish washing was done in an enamel bowl on a side table in the corner of the living room; and water was heated in a kettle on the coal fire there.

When I knew her Granny Bowen always looked very stern; her sight was poor, she wore glasses and during cold weather she frequently wore a hat over her sparse hair in the house; her voice was sharp, but she had a soft centre and a kind heart and always made us feel welcome. Her home was near a public house called The Engine Inn beside a level crossing of the Great Western Railway. A signal box stood just inside the gates of this crossing and the signal man was Charlie Rendall, married to Lizzie's cousin Dorothy. They lived beside some of my school friends on an estate called The Garden Suburb near St Mary's church. From the age of ten, when I was at Granny Bowen's, every now and then I visited Charlie in the signal box and he would show me how he moved the levers to keep the trains running on the GWR.

Occasionally I called on Granny Bowen in the early morning to find Muriel dressed in a large pinafore, with her hair in dinkie curlers under a fashionable turban, busily cleaning the house with a mop, a tin of Mansion Polish, and a yellow duster. She was a tall, thin energetic bony lady, with a sharply angled jaw, capable of doing the most wonderful ironing on the large table in their living room, with flat irons heated on the coal fire. While she did so I would sit and talk to her, admiring her skill.

I liked using Granny Bowen's home as a base during school holidays because some of my school friends lived near her in New Street, one of them was Maud Williams who was in my class and also attended St Mary's church. When we first came to live in Caterham I met Maud's younger sister Brenda. She was married to an Englishman called John. and they had two daughters Our small son Malcolm began to attend the same primary school in Whyteleafe and one day as I stood waiting to pick him up after school Maud was standing beside me. Although we had not met for twelve years I recognised her immediately she told me that my school friends

Maureen and Tony were married and living in The Garden Suburb near St Mary's church and they had a daughter. Maud said she too was married and lived in Llanelly with her family and since then we have sent each other Christmas cards and met at Brenda's home in Caterham.

SADNESS

I was unaware that the bombing of London and the strain of being separated from us and our father had begun to seriously affect our mother's health. She came to Wales that winter to attend the funeral of Nanny Maloney, coming to Burry Port beforehand. It was lovely to see her though we were sad to hear about Nanny. It was snowing hard and getting dark as she kissed me goodbye and I stood watching until she disappeared from sight in the direction of the station to take the train to Aberkenfig to join her in-laws and my Dad, who was on compassionate leave from the army.

Suffering from exhaustion after Nanny's funeral, she went back to her childhood home in Cymmer to stay with Bessie, and rest. Nights in Lloyds Terrace were not disturbed by bombing raids. Sleeping in the bedroom above the front door she hoped to regain her health.

To help pay the mortgage on our home in Edgware my father got leave from the army to arrange for our house to be rented to a bombed out family. A few weeks later he came to Burry Port and took us to Cymmer to pick up our mother and we went on the train to Aberkenfig to see his brother Griff. While there we went on a bus ride and on the journey our parents fell out about money. I comforted my mother who was in tears because my father had spent the money meant to pay the mortgage. Oh dear!

Now that Janet was back home in Edgware Lizzie and Jim paid for me to have piano lessons but I never enjoyed it even though I practised for an hour on the organ after school, every day. After a few months, much to my relief, it was decided that I was not a born pianist; I am practically tone deaf! The only tune I remember learning to play was 'The Blue Bells of Scotland', which seems rather prophetic since I married David who is very proud to be a Scot.

A Mrs Howells who lived in a bungalow in Colby Road took in a little five year old evacuee called Sadie and asked Lizzie if I would play with her after school. She was a dear little girl but she did not stay long: she missed her mother too much and could not sleep at night unless Mrs. Howells held her hand, and within a couple of weeks her mother came and took her back to London.

LLOYDS TERRACE, CYMMER

In January 1942 auntie Mary became pregnant, left the Army and returned to her childhood home in Lloyds Terrace With Bessie and family and our mother already in residence Lizzie took us to Cymmer more often than ever. Occasionally when we got off the train there, we called to see my grandfather's diminutive youngest sister great aunt Gwen Thomas, a spinster who lived alone in a tiny house in Cymmer valley. She used to go to Cowbridge to visit the Thomas family. One of my cousins told me recently that when she was young auntie Gwen had a proposal of marriage in Cowbridge but her father, Charles Thomas, would not hear of it and went to fetch her, telling her there was work for her to do at home in Glyncorrwg. When I knew her she was extremely garrulous with a very mobile tongue, patently obvious because she had no teeth. I was aware of this because she did not wear dentures! Most adults of past generations lost their teeth in their twenties, and I became conscious of the unusual fact that unlike all her brothers and sisters my mother still had all her teeth and they were perfect.

I wish I had paid attention to great auntie Gwen's chatter, because she could tell a good tale. She never seemed to stop talking! Indeed it is a common characteristic in my family on both sides and perhaps in Welsh people generally. Gran Hill used to say 'we all have the gift of the gab', and the ability to 'talk the hind leg off a donkey.'

One day when Terry was seven and I was ten we were surprised to see our father at Lloyds Terrace when we arrived. He had been staying there with my mother and was about to rejoin his army unit. Because he was late leaving he walked very fast to the railway station and Terry and I had to run to keep up with him; but he missed his train and he told us to go back to the house and say nothing. But, as usual, Terry blurted it out as soon as he saw Mummy and she cried. My Dad told Terry years later that he was forced to spend three days in the Guard House for being AWOL (absent without leave) for 24 hours.

When it drew near to the time of the birth of her baby, Mary's waters broke and Bessie ran down Lloyds Terrace to telephone for an ambulance. While she did so Mummy got up out of bed to look after Mary and then Bessie accompanied her in the ambulance to the hospital in Neath. All the way there she kept telling Mary not to make a fuss, but her baby Michael would not wait. He came quickly into this world and was born in the ambulance as they arrived at the hospital, and Bessie had to run in to get help.

CHAPTER ELEVEN

Tuberculosis

On our frequent visits to Cymmer I often found Bessie's youngest child, three year old Gillian, playing on my mother's bed and unknown to Terry and me one day Gillian took ill and died suddenly, revealing the dreadful truth that my mother was seriously ill with tuberculosis and had infected her. At that time there was no cure for this killer disease and children and young people were extremely vulnerable, so patients were isolated as quickly as possible and from the day that Gillian died, we were forbidden to see our mother. It must have been a desperately harrowing time for all concerned. Poor Bessie, poor Mummy and most of all poor little Gillian. She was a sweet child.

My mother had to go to a sanatorium which was a secure place for people suffering from tuberculosis, she was admitted to the Cymla hospital in Neath prior to doing so. Bessie and her family moved to a home of their own and Gran Hill at the age of sixty eight, now almost totally blind owing to glaucoma, decided to go home to Lloyds Terrace from Staffordshire to comfort her grieving family, and was brought there by one of her nephews who ran a transport and haulage business in Glamorgan. Mary, her youngest daughter, made up a bed with a commode for Gran in the parlour at Lloyds Terrace.

SEPARATION

During my mother's short stay at the Cymla hospital she was allowed to get up and dress in the afternoons and while she was there, she knitted me a doll in WAAF (Women's Auxiliary Air Force) uniform which I treasured for years. Her sisters and many cousins visited her often but my father only visited her once and although they had their photograph taken together for us in the garden there, they both looked unhappy and were sitting apart because of their fear of tuberculosis. Soon after that she was transferred to a sanatorium called Craig yr Nos, situated near Brecon in the beautiful countryside of the Black Mountains, which had previously been the home of the famous opera singer Adelina Patti.

In 1980 Craig yr Nos, which is often described as a castle, had not been used as a sanatorium for many years and it was suggested as a possible home for the Prince of Wales and his bride Princess Diana, but they turned it down.

My mother's cousin Miles kindly transported her by car from the Cymla to Burry Port for her to see us before she went to Craig yr Nos, and we took the day off school. In the afternoon an ambulance arrived to take her to the sanatorium and the driver said only one adult and one child could accompany her. So it was agreed that Terry and auntie Lizzie would go with her and I had to be brave and accept that there was no room for me. Hiding my misery I said goodbye to her with a lump in my throat and as they boarded the ambulance I ran down Cwm Ifor Road choking back the tears. When I reached Church Hill heading for Granny Bowen's home for consolation, I turned and with blurred vision saw the ambulance disappearing in the direction of Llanelly.

CRAIG YR NOS

Mummy was a patient in Craig yr Nos for almost a year during which time we could not see her but I wrote and received occasional letters from her. She sent me a black Mammie rag doll she won in a raffle and though I was far too old for dolls it had pride of place in my bedroom. In the spring of 1943 we picked bunches of multicoloured primroses from the orchard and Lizzie helped pack them in a moss lined cardboard box to post to her and once a fortnight she left Terry and me in Swansea with Jim's family while she visited her.

For many years I possessed one of Mummy's leather handbags and a diary she kept in Craig yr Nos recording how she pined for us and our Dad who often promised to visit her but seldom did. She must have felt very lonely and deep down what happened affected me a lot. However Terry and I had become used to life in Burry Port without electricity: we were settled in school with good friends and not greatly disturbed by the war and we sounded like natives, speaking Welsh at times, and we could sing the Welsh national anthem with gusto.

Lizzie allowed us to have a pretty long haired short tailed black cat called Kitty, who frequently attempted to follow me to school. She was loveable and one evening she went missing. The next morning Terry woke to hear her crying outside his bedroom window where the trees from the woods hung over the roof and when he looked out he saw Kitty sitting in the guttering trying to get into his bedroom. Uncle Jim had of course gone to work, so Lizzie put up a ladder but, being diminutive, when she climbed up she could not reach Kitty. We went to school in great distress. But when we returned in the afternoon, all was well. We were delighted to find

Kitty purring happily in front of the fire. She had found her own way down to the ground.

The coal man called periodically delivering a ton of coal and because the lane was narrow he could not get his horse and cart up to Rhandir Delyn and he was forced to carry up each hundred-weight sack on his back and empty it just inside the garden gate, while Lizzie stood counting them. Because Jim was at work she then fetched a wheelbarrow almost as big as herself, and gradually with our assistance she transported it all to the coal shed in the back yard. It was a hard task. I disliked getting dirty but the more Terry was covered in coal dust, the more he enjoyed it!

AUNTS AND UNCLES

In the late Spring of 1943, Lizzie and Jim planned to take us to Ellesmere Port to visit Gran Hill's sister Louie. We were excited at the prospect of a long train journey and a few days off school, but as the bombing continued they decided to go without us. Instead, as Tom was on leave from the Fleet Air Arm, he and Addie came to look after us and we loved it. Leaving Addie to cook dinner Tom came to church with us on Sunday morning and because Terry was a choir boy I was delighted to have Tom's full attention in church. I was so proud to walk beside him in his bell bottom trousers, and my friends were green with envy and many came up and touched his sailor collar for luck. At breakfast one morning Addie told us that Kitty the cat had caught a mouse in their bedroom during the night. We had never seen one and would not believe it. She said 'Uncle Tom has thrown it under a tree in the orchard,' so we rushed out to discover the so-called mouse was a bat. They give me nightmares yet!

Later that year Mary came to look after us while Lizzie and Jim went to visit Addie who was living alone in Oxford. One morning Mary was bathing baby Michael in a tub in front of the fire when Terry accidentally knocked it over and saturated the rugs. It took three days to dry them out! There were no tumble dryers then! Mary was young and energetic with a quick wit and repartee, well read, full of quotations, and knew many poetical works. She often quoted Rudyard Kipling's 'If' to us. She must have had quite a good education and she called a spade a spade. She told me how babies came into the world and said Gran Hill never told any of her daughters the facts of life. They found them out when they got married! Mary was twenty years younger than Lizzie and taller than all her sisters. She gave us little treats of comics and sweets and took us to the Italian ice cream parlour in Station Road where we sat at a little table and had milkshakes with a straw. We had never done that and found it very exciting, for there was virtually no ice cream during the war.

Given the lack of sanitation, electricity and hot water it was hard work caring for a baby in Rhandir Delyn. Mary encouraged us to use the toilet at school as often as possible so that she did not have to dig a hole in the garden for the sewage! She was nervous at night and made sure the back door was locked even during the day which was a problem when we needed to use Lizzie's toilet. It was a lonely place and she was not accustomed to it. At the time I never gave it a thought but I would not care to live there today. One morning a telegraph boy brought a telegram and Mary was frightened to open it but it said only that her husband Jim was coming on leave. We were all delighted to see him. He was a great bookworm and card player and when he was not nursing his baby he liked sitting on Lizzie's balcony in the sunshine, reading her classic novels, and in the evenings when baby Michael was asleep we all played cards together.

Great aunt Tilly, one of Gran Hill's cousins, lived in a small terrace house in Burry Port. Tiny and very dainty, with her white hair in the Edwardian style, she visited Rhandir Delyn occasionally, bringing her knitting and wearing long black old fashioned clothes. She had no children and had been a widow for many years. Her home was absolutely full of Victoriana and I had a feeling of claustrophobia whenever I entered it. One day she had a stroke and was taken to Bryntyrien hospital in Llanelly. Lizzie took me to see her there and when she died Lizzie and Mary had the job of disposing of her possessions. I helped Mary throw out many things which were regarded as junk then, but today would be considered valuable. However, we did keep some beautiful paperweights which are now distributed among the family. Mary told me that Tilly had married a man by the name of Samuels, who was a great deal older than her, and when they left by train on their honeymoon, Tilly sat in the only vacant seat in the compartment and her husband had to stand. Seeing her sitting there another passenger rebuked her saying 'You should give your seat to your father!'

Meanwhile Addie decided to leave Oxford and return to Cymmer until the end of the war, so Lizzie and Jim made arrangements for some of her furniture to be transported to Rhandir Delyn for safe keeping. In due course a sideboard and armchairs arrived, which were put in the parlour, and a tallboy and a wardrobe, damaged as it was carried up our rutted lane, was put in my bedroom. One afternoon when we came home from Sunday school we discovered uncle Tom and another sailor sitting there. They were on embarkation leave and had been to see Tom's mother. They stayed for tea with us and ate some of Lizzie's black currant tart and we enjoyed every minute of their stay.

SUNDAY SCHOOL OUTINGS

Because families were unable to go away for holidays in wartime Sunday school outings to the seaside were great adventures for all children. Early in the morning, Terry and I, carrying a packed lunch and pocket money, would congregate excitedly at Burry Port station with our friends, teachers and some parents to catch a train to spend the day at Ferry Side, Porthcawl, Mumbles, Barry Island or Carmarthen. At Ferry Side, because the sea was so near, it seemed as if we stepped off the train almost on to the beach. What a thrill that was, with Llanstephan castle on the horizon just across the estuary. Barry Island and Porthcawl had large fun fairs which were very entertaining if the weather was poor. Mumbles was my favourite resort: it had its own very special charm which still exists today and we approached it by tram which ran along the coast from the train at Swansea.

On Friday nights before bed, uncle Jim Ogborn gave us both a penny pocket money. Lizzie bought our sweets and gave us three pence for the children's Saturday afternoon cinema and, intermittently, my Dad sent money for our keep and occasionally came to see us in his army uniform. He was now a sergeant in REME and wore a regimental cap. He had little in common with Lizzie and Jim so whenever possible he liked sitting listening to the wireless in their front room and Terry and I would join him there. His favourite programme was called ITMA, a very popular wartime programme with the comedian Tommy Handley. Sometimes Dad looked very sad and once I found him sitting there crying. Terry comforted him while I made him a cup of tea and once on a Sunday he went to the little Catholic church in Burry Port. Terry and I liked walking up our lane with him and drinking from the natural spring in the bank at the head of the little stream where we might see kingfishers, and then according to the season go on to climb the old oak tree, count the lambs in the fields or collect acorns; then we would call at the farm for a glass of milk straight from a cow. Just once in a blue moon those same cows would wander down the lane in the early morning and if uncle Jim had accidentally left the gate open when he went to work they would cause havoc in the garden until Lizzie chased them out.

Now that Gran Hill was back in her own home she had many visitors and when we arrived there with Lizzie we often found her still in bed. She was totally blind and when we greeted her she felt our faces with her hands firing questions at us while she did so. She was a real character: her mind was razor sharp and she was much loved by her large family and seldom stopped talking. We would leave her sitting in her carver chair talking to Lizzie while we went out to play with the local children on the mountain side. One of her greatest pleasures was listening to the wireless. Before the advent of national television, every one except the blind had to pay an annual licence fee for a wireless and she fully expected her dinner to be on the dining table as the pips went for the one o' clock news and auntie Mary, bless her, always managed to achieve this. Gran loved her food and spent her day crocheting while listening to the wireless or talking to friends and family.

When her sister in law, great aunt Bessie, was there they spoke Welsh together. She frequently spent the day with Gran, sitting at

Great Aunt Bessie.

the dining table with her spectacles on the end of her nose, knitting long white sea socks for wartime sailors. When we arrived on a visit she would invoke my aid to hold the hanks of wool for her to wind into balls. A little lady, grey haired and absent minded, she was probably around sixty years of age, which seemed extremely old to me. If neighbours called in to see Gran while she was there she stopped knitting and pushed her spectacles to the top of her head. When they departed she would ask 'Where are my glasses?' and we children would pretend to help her find them, knowing all the time they were balanced on top of her head. Then auntie Mary would appear and tell her where they were!

Once Lizzie took us to visit her cousin Louie who lived in a bungalow near the vast beach in Pendine in Carmarthenshire. I did not know then that it was the same beach where my father had been with great uncle Will, to watch Parry Thomas testing his racing car; and Jim and Amy Mollison, the solo air aces, had flown from there too. Also, during the second world war some of the manoeuvres for the D Day landings in France were secretly rehearsed on Pendine Sands. This historic event, which eventually culminated in the end of the second world war, took place on 6th June 1944 when thousands of British and allied troops landed on the Normandy coast of France.

CHAPTER TWELVE

Return to Edgware

One day in the spring of 1943 auntie Lizzie told us our mother was leaving the sanatorium and coming to Rhandir Delyn. We were extremely thrilled. I was convinced she must be well again. Her cousin Miles drove Lizzie and me to Brecon and while Lizzie went to fetch her I waited in the car outside Craig yr Nos. I was so happy I wanted to cry and it was wonderful to see her after such a long time. I held her hand all the way back to Burry Port and later that day she sat with her arms around Terry and me in the front room of Rhandir Delyn. It was magic. I felt as if we were in heaven. She told us she had decided to take us back home to London to live with her, because even though our Dad was in the army he would be allowed to sleep at home to help her to look after us. She thought the war was coming to an end and she would soon get her strength back. What did it matter that I was about to sit the eleven plus exam at school with a strong possibility of going to Llanelly Grammar School? I would be with my mother again and that to me was the most important thing in the world. I was almost eleven and Terry was eight and a half years old.

Dad got compassionate leave to escort us home to Edgware on the train and Addie came to help us settle in. It took many hours to reach London because the train took the long route through Gloucester and kept stopping for long periods. We grew hungry and thirsty and Terry cried a lot, already missing Lizzie and friends in Burry Port, my father kept taking him for walks in the train corridor. We reached Paddington station in the early evening to find lots of sandbags in the street outside, and when my Dad tried to get a taxi driver to take us the ten miles home to Edgware they all refused, afraid to risk being caught in an air raid. So we travelled on the underground train followed by a bus ride and a ten minute walk. I could see that Mummy looked very weary and she collapsed into bed when we reached home.

After four years in Wales, it was strange to be back in Edgware. It did not feel like home any more: the bombed out family who had been living in our house had removed or broken most of our family possessions, including our verandah which they had used as fire wood.

Next morning my father returned to his barracks and while my mother and Addie were busy in the house Terry and I went out to look at the concrete street shelter and discovered a large bin with the words 'Pig Swill' near our gate, in which residents put their food scraps. All the children were at school and the houses looked drab and neglected with blackout curtains at the windows. Barrage balloons were still in the sky above de Havillands aircraft factory and from the bedroom window at the back of our house we could see Anderson shelters in our neighbours' gardens.

We couldn't find any of our old toys or games and in the afternoon, searching for something to play with, and unknown to our mother, we found a set of darts in the garage and decided to throw them to each other on the lawn in the front garden to see how far they would travel. How stupid of me! I should have known better, for almost at once a dart landed in the back of my hand. I rushed into the house and Addie washed the wound under the kitchen tap. After a couple of hours my hand began to throb and by the time my Dad returned from his barracks that evening, my arm was swelling rapidly. He had the presence of mind to walk me down to our local hospital where they gave me the necessary treatment, and told him that had I waited until morning, I might well have developed blood poisoning. I wore a sling for a few days and fully recovered. After a couple of weeks Addie returned to Wales and our Dad slept at home, going to his barracks in uniform every day.

TUBERCULOSIS AGAIN

It was good to see my friend Janet who still lived three doors away but she and her parents and all the other neighbours did not visit us any more. I soon began to realise why. They all thought my mother still had tuberculosis and were frightened of becoming infected with the disease. Auntie Winnie was in Wales with little Ronald so we had no visitors. There was some discussion between my parents about my attending a grammar school but it was finally decided I would go to the local secondary school so that I could get home quickly to help my Mum: I missed my Welsh friends and the country life; I loathed the school, the pupils, and the dinners they provided which I rarely ate; and Janet was still in the junior school. At weekends we did enjoy going to Sunday school at St Lawrence Whitchurch and sitting in the box pews in the church. Then every Friday after school it was my job to do the weekly shopping for our family at the butcher's and grocer's stores in Mollison Way. Our ration books were registered. there. I hated doing it and it took such a long time. On one side of the grocer's shop were the dry foods like sugar, tinned food and jam preserves; on the other side the cold foods like butter, cheese and eggs. Everyone had to queue up and all the food had to be weighed, measured or counted according to how many portions were allowed per family and ration books were marked accordingly. Then I went on to the butcher's and the green grocer's.

I became extremely hungry while queuing up for the shopping every Friday and began to suffer from severe headaches. When I got home with the groceries and told my Mum she would not believe me. Both she and my Dad said 'Children do not get headaches!' but I did, and it was possibly the start of migraine from which I suffered for many years.

When my Dad did not come home in time to make our evening meal, I made it. Mummy's appetite was extremely poor and I tried to cut very thin slices of bread and butter for her. Goodness knows what she ate at lunch time for there were no Meals on Wheels in those days. I loved our parents, we both did, but I hated living in Edgware then, worrying about my mother and I had no one to turn to. For, although my father came home every night, he had no time to talk to me.

Perhaps it's just as well that my little brother and I had no idea how seriously ill Mummy was. I noticed how red her cheeks were and how thin she was becoming. She had always been fastidious and house proud but now she was very lethargic and began to get up later and later, doing less and less, spending most of her time lying down, coughing day and night and using a small blue bottle to spit into. A nurse called regularly and the local authority provided a cleaner who did some of her house work, but Mummy used to say, 'No one cleans my corners like I do.'

I now know something of how she felt, for like my mother I too, cannot do my own housework because for the past few years I have been unable to walk more than a few steps at a time owing to a spinal decompression which failed. At first I was blessed with the help of a good friend who came for two hours every week to help me. She was very supportive, kind and helpful and tried to sort out the chaos because David had had to learn to do the cooking and the shopping too. I became very frustrated when things had to be left undone. Imagine trying to do a week's housework in two hours?

One day I told my helpful friend what my mother had said about her 'corners' and that I now knew what she meant. My friend took umbrage at my remarks and never came to see me again and sadly, we have gone our separate ways. We had a maxim at school 'Think Before You Speak, and Speak Not All You Think.' Fortunately, we now have a home help called Stella and a Czech au pair called Martina, who does our washing and ironing; they are both wonderful and have become our friends.

AIR RAIDS

In 1943 Greenwich Mean Time was moved not just one hour, to British Summer Time, but two hours, to Double Summer Time which meant that daylight lasted long into the night that summer to help the war effort. That summer when there was no air raid I could read in bed until almost midnight when there was no air raid but sometimes raids lasted all night and. I often had a premonition that a raid was imminent, and could easily recognise the distinctive throb of German bomber planes.

On the way to school after a raid we would find lots of shrapnel in the streets and occasionally passed a bomb site; thankfully we lived ten miles from the heart of London. If my Dad was home during a raid I sometimes joined him looking out of our sitting room window, watching the search lights seeking German bomber planes among the barrage balloons in the night sky, while all around us the sound of anti-air craft guns vibrated and flashed. making a tremendous din.

Occasionally I spent the night with Janet, sleeping with her in the Morrison shelter in their sitting room. Her grandmother who used to live with them had died and if there was a raid her parents joined us and we played board games until the 'All Clear' siren.

At night if Terry and I were asleep in bed and my Dad was not at home when the siren went off my Mum woke us up to go down stairs and lie under the dining table until the All Clear siren sounded,but she remained upstairs in bed. When this happened I found it very frightening listening to the enemy aeroplanes flying overhead, dropping their bombs, accompanied by the gun fire.

As autumn approached the coal man filled the bunker in our back garden and every day before leaving for the barracks my Dad lit a coal fire with newspaper and firewood, first removing the coal dust and ash to put in our dustbin which created a lot of dust. I could write my name on the mantelpiece every morning so before I went to school I hoovered and dusted the room: in the twenty first century I still call our refuse collectors 'Dustmen,' a legacy from those days when every one had a coal fire and consequently, every week the bins were full of coal dust

As the nights began to draw in my mother grew weaker and she told us she had written to Addie to ask her if she would come and help look after us. On the day we expected her, just a few weeks before Christmas, I sat looking out of our sitting room window but there was no sign of her. It began to get dark and my mother said with resignation, 'Never mind, she is not coming, after all.' Then suddenly I could see her. How happy we were, and what a relief it must have been for our mother.

FEARLESS ADDIE

I did not realise just how brave aunt Addie was to come and stay in a home with someone who had tuberculosis. In 1944 there were no antibiotics or drugs of any kind to cure this dreadful disease. Addie was marvellous, loving and kind. She took charge of everything in our home and we discovered she was very house proud and quite strict about our behaviour. We used to tease her, calling her 'School Ma'am', and 'Madam Polish', but even so, we loved her dearly.

My father continued to come home from the barracks at night and often slept on the settee in the sitting room. He was probably reluctant to share my mother's bed and now I realise why and ask myself, Who could blame him? Daytime bombing ceased for a while and every now and again when he had a day's leave, still wearing his army uniform, he would take us to London to show us famous buildings. We visited Trafalgar Square and Piccadilly Circus, which he told us is the centre of the earth and I was amazed and a little proud when he paused and saluted as we walked past the Cenotaph in Whitehall.

I recall little of Christmas Day 1943 except that Addie cooked our Christmas dinner and Dad carried Mummy down stairs to the sitting room where she lay on the settee all day. In the New Year before getting washed and dressed we visited her in her bedroom every morning and one day she was cross with me because she noticed that I was wearing my vest and liberty bodice under my

Dear aunt Addie.

night dress Now little girls no longer wear liberty bodices probably because we all have central heating.

When I came home from school I always went to see my Mum and one day Addie told me there was a visitor upstairs and I found an attractive young woman I did not recognise sitting beside her bed: it was my father's cousin Dilys. She and her parents had been living in Colwyn Bay for three years and Dilys was about to get married to a Welshman she had met there. She said that uncle Will and auntie Beat had returned to Euston to take over another hotel, because the Evans Hotel had been severely bomb damaged. They too, must have thought the war was coming to and end.

Quite soon after that Mummy asked me to buy her some black currant lozenges from the chemist and gave me her purse to take some money to buy them and I took an extra shilling. Of course she found out. I knew she would. I did it deliberately, because I wanted her undivided attention. Naturally I got it when I returned but she forgave me. Many years later I told Addie what I had done and the reason why.

A few weeks later in the spring our Mum became very ill and our family doctor called every day. Uncle Tom in his Fleet Air Arm uniform came on leave for a few days at Easter and one night we had a very heavy air raid; my mother and Addie remained upstairs in their beds and my Dad put Terry and me on a mattress in the cupboard under the stairs and he and Tom stood at our open front door watching the searchlights and we all listened to the gunfire and the sound of exploding bombs.

During the day time Tom visited the Dixon family, he also spent a lot of time sitting with my mother at her open bedroom windows cracking jokes with the neighbours as they passed, which made

Mummy laugh a lot. He cheered us all immensely, and lifted our spirits before he returned to his aircraft carrier on Easter Monday.

BEREAVEMENT

We were on school holidays and the Tuesday after Easter was my twelfth birthday. Addie told me that my mother's favourite flowers were anemones and she suggested I go and buy her some from the florist in Mollison Way. So that's what I did and Mummy loved them. Four days later on the Saturday afternoon, the 15th April 1944, I heard the terrible noise of her struggling for breath. Our family doctor was called and Terry and I were sent to the cinema. I still remember the film we saw, which upsets me even to this day when it is shown on TV, for I knew instinctively that when we returned my mother would be dead and that is exactly what happened.

The following day Addie took us both to our parents' bedroom to kiss our mother goodbye. It was extremely traumatic for me. I wish I had never done it. I felt empty inside and afterwards my little brother stood outside our parents' bedroom door and asked Addie 'Who will be my Mummy now?' and suddenly I felt again an enormous lump in my throat, but I could not cry.

On the day of her funeral Addie gave us a little card which said 'In Loving Remembrance', and Terry and I put our names on it and she attached it to a little bunch of forget-me-not flowers. Lizzie and Jim with Emily came up from Wales and uncle Arthur was there. Our house was full of flowers from our neighbours and that night I slept very little because I shared a bed with Addie and Emily who talked almost all night long. It was a very sad time especially for Terry and me.......... We were overwhelmed. Next day our Dad walked with us to see the flowers on Mummy's grave and within a few days he took us on the tube train to Paddington station where he put us on the train for Burry Port, in the care of the guard, and he returned to his regiment.

Our beloved mother lies buried in an unmarked grave in the churchyard of the historic St Lawrence Whitchurch in Cannons Park. She was thirty three years old. I have only two personal mementoes of her: one is a trinket pot with a silver top which used to sit on her dressing table and now sits on my Welsh dresser; the other memento is a pretty little bone china Peace mug from the 1914-18 Great War which she was given at school when she was seven years old.

Occasionally through the years I have visited her grave with my family. The last time, when I could still walk, was in the early spring of 1999 when Caterham parish church arranged a coach trip to St Lawrence's. Beforehand I wrote to the vicar there and he arranged for the guide to show me the exact spot after we had toured the church, which has a 16th century tower with an extension built by the Duke of Chandos in 1715, with box pews, where Terry and I sat for Sunday school lessons when we were children. On a balcony above the nave is the Ducal pew, like a theatre box with its own fireplace. The Duke employed the composer Frederick Handel and behind the altar is an organ Handel used to play. A friend accompanied me to my mother's graveside that day where I placed a bunch of anemones. I bought a St Lawrence mug being sold to help with funds for the upkeep of the church and it stands today among my commemorative mugs.

CHAPTER THIRTEEN

Safe from Doodle Bugs

In June 1944 when Terry and I were safely back in Burry Port Hitler began bombing London with V1 flying bombs known as doodle bugs. They were deadly and very destructive so Janet's mother brought her back to stay with us in Burry port. In bed on that first night Janet told me how in broad daylight she had seen a doodle bug stop dead in the sky near her home and fall without a sound, hitting a house in the next street and totally destroying it with an enormous explosion, leaving a vast crater. A few weeks later we heard that Hitler was sending even more powerful rockets over London and the south of England, called V2s .

One day we were playing after school at the bottom of our lane when we met about a dozen tall good looking, extremely friendly Yankee soldiers with extraordinary long legs, wearing very smart uniforms. They were based in the adjoining village of Pembrey, where my father was occasionally based when he was visiting us. They gave us chewing gum and chocolate, and tins of chocolate powder and cigarettes called Lucky Strike to all the grownups they met along Colby Road! They were the first foreigners most British people had ever seen, for in those days before package holidays the average person had never been abroad and very few members of the population travelled over seas except for those who fought abroad in wars.

That summer Lizzie took us all to Cymmer to spend our school holidays, one night Janet cried in bed because she missed her mother and I told her she was lucky, for she still had a mother to cry for. We were fortunate to belong to a family with a large number of loving aunts. Leaving Terry and Janet with auntie Mary and Gran I went on my own to stay with Bessie and family and then on to Sarn to stay with great aunt Sue and Winnie and her children Ronald and his baby sister Linda. They were all lovely to me.

Many years later when our son Malcolm was a boy we had a family gathering for a wedding in Sarn and one evening at dusk my cousin Ronald and I went together to visit great aunt Sue whom neither of us had seen for many years. When we knocked on her front door she appeared from her back garden and peering at us in the gathering gloom she recognised me instantly, saying 'Kathleen!' Even though it was more than twenty years since we had met, at that moment time stood still and I was a child again.

ABERGWYNFI

I always enjoyed the short bus ride from Cymmer to the mining village of Abergwynfi to visit my mother's sister Emily. Just a year younger than Lizzie she was a widow with two children, Peggy and Jack, who were much older than us. Emily wore her hair in a bun, rode a bicycle and kept a fish and chip shop attached to her home. She was known in the village as 'Auntie Fish' or 'Mrs Jones the Fish'. Her house was on three floors. At the bottom there were a kitchen and living room, with an outside loo but no bathroom. Behind the shop on the main street was a well furnished sitting room which I think was never used, and on the top floor were three bedrooms.

Emily's children still lived with her. My cousin Peggy, who was the same age as my auntie Mary, was married to a sailor called Va and they had two infant sons called David and Douglas whom I liked playing with. I enjoyed sitting in Emily's back garden looking down the mountainside watching the activities of the bowling green in the valley below, beside a school and playground and the terminus of the local railway where I could watch steam engines shunting up and down. Best of all I liked staying the night there so that I could help in the fish and chip shop, working the potato chipping machine and serving Auntie Fish's friendly customers. When you are hungry there's nothing quite like freshly cooked fish and chips seasoned with salt and vinegar and wrapped in newspaper. It really gets the salivary glands working!

Peggy's husband Va had been invalided out of the navy when he was torpedoed by the Germans. Consequently he was often home when I was there. He and Peggy were very happy together and he was a great tease. One evening he escorted the two of us on a short journey by bus to the cinema in the little town of Maesteg. It was dark when we left the cinema and they decided to make the return journey by train. With practically no one else on board we sat in an empty compartment and just before we entered the tunnel under the mountain to Abergwynfi, Va shut the windows to shut out the smoke and noise from the steam engine and drew the blinds. Then to my amazement with the remarkable alacrity of a sailor he shinned up on to the luggage rack and removed the dim blue light bulbs, leaving us in total darkness for a short time, which made Peggy and me scream with hysterical laughter. Her laughter sounded just like my mother's!

While I was staying with them Peggy's brother Jack, a handsome lad aged about eighteen, decided to have a bath in a tin tub in the kitchen before going out for the evening, courting the girls. Afterwards to reach the stairs to get to his bedroom two floors above for clean clothes, he leapt across the living room where we were all sitting and as he did so he shouted, particularly for my benefit, 'Close your eyes!' but I didn't! He was stark naked!

Armed with buckets and spades that summer of 1944 Terry, Janet and I, accompanied by Lizzie and sometimes Addie, went down the old tramway to the seaside, to dig up cockles from the sands and collect mussels lying near the lighthouse at the end of the harbour. We always returned tired out but starving hungry. Yet I did not eat shellfish. I couldn't bear to hear them crying in the pot as they were being boiled on Lizzie's oil stove!

NEW SCHOOL

I thoroughly enjoyed my school days at the Burry Port coeducational secondary school. I wore a navy gym slip and a white blouse. I made some new friends and became a prefect among a mixed class of 30 girls and boys. The teaching staff were pleasant and I began to grieve less for my mother. I excelled in English literature, history and poetry and every week at the end of his lesson the geography master read a chapter of 'Just William' by Richmal Crompton which lifted my spirits! Mr Evans the Welsh master, who knew Lizzie, taught us English speaking children his native language and welcomed me and two of my friends to his classroom every lunch time. The English teacher Miss Greville taught P.E. too and gave me some of her own books to read at home and allowed me to opt out of gym and hockey, playing only net ball and rounders. Janet returned to Edgware a short time later, and I had my bedroom to myself again.

While the boys in our class learnt woodwork, we girls learnt domestic science. Cookery was one of my favourite subjects. However, because of food rationing we never learnt how to cook meat. To protect our uniform we were encouraged to bring an apron to wear and Lizzie found me some very dainty white pinafores edged with broderie anglais. Years later I realised they had been my mother's aprons when she was in service as a parlour maid in Wellington Square. We concentrated on fruit desserts and pastries which we took home to eat afterwards. Towards the end of the autumn term my best friend Maureen and I had became so adept at making mince pies and vol-au-vents with rough puff pastry that we were excused certain lessons to make them for Miss Rowlands the Domestic Science mistress and for Mr. Thomas the Head Master, who provided us with the ingredients. Many years later, it was always my pleasure to make them for my family at Christmastime.

In the spring of 1945 my mother's cousin Nellie James and her son, fourteen year old Greville, came on a visit to Rhandir Delyn. While I attempted to pick some primroses in the orchard for her to take home to Cwmafan, Greville a handsome lad with dark hair kept trying to put a grasshopper down the back of my dress. All great fun! I showed him how to play three balls on the wall in the back yard and then we went picking bluebells together in the woods behind the orchard.

The second time Greville and I met was forty year later when my husband David and I were on holiday staying with auntie Bessie in Aberafan One night I asked her again about our family history, and she took me to meet Greville. I knocked on the front door of his house in Cwmafan and a sash window opened above my head and a man with thinning hair stuck his head out, and I looked up and said 'I am looking for my cousin Greville,' and he replied, in a strong Welsh accent, 'I am Greville!'

He and his wife Marion, made us all welcome, and she made tea while we admired their collection of Welsh love spoons adorning the chimney breast in their cottage and Greville showed me the large portrait of our great grandfather Charles Thomas, as an old man with an enormous white beard. Later he took us across the road to Michaelstone church the vicar let us look at the parish records and then Greville showed us the gravestones of our ancestors by the name of Peters including of course our great great grandfather John Peters.

EPILEPSY

As children Terry and I had grown accustomed to the frequent sound emanating from Lizzie and Jim's bedroom in the dead of night. We often heard her calling him by name, accompanied by a slapping sound and heavy breathing. Lizzie always maintained these disturbed nights were because Jim was allergic to certain foods and it was not until 1948 that they sought medical advice, only to discover that he had suffered all his married life from nocturnal epilepsy.

For many years, this little lady with only one kidney had coped with this problem in somewhat primitive conditions. In the spring of 1945 life was made somewhat easier for them both with the installation of electricity, but they still had no vacuum cleaner and continued to cook on the oil stove. I began to help with the housework, cleaning my own bedroom every week with a mop and duster, doing the washing up and the shopping. There was talk in the family that Lizzie and Jim would adopt us, but it never came to anything and I doubt that my father would have agreed to it.

VE DAY

I was thirteen years old in May 1945 the War in Europe ended, throwing the whole of the United Kingdom into party mood and our church bells rang for the first time in six years. To celebrate VE (Victory in Europe) Day a fete was held on my school playing fields attended by a great many happy people. Newsreels at the cinema were full of jubilant scenes in the streets of London.

From that day every Sunday we heard our church bells ringing reminding us to go to church and Terry and I became confirmed members of the Church in Wales. Two of my school friends, Tony and Raymond became bell ringers and one Sunday morning I went up into the belfry to watch them doing it.

One day I fainted during a maths lesson at school and the master, Mr Griffiths, took me home in his car, so there must surely have been some relaxation in petrol rationing although the second world war still continued against Japan.

That summer Terry's friend John Edwards asked us both to help his father with the hay making and at the end of the day we returned to the farm sitting on top of the hay cart; that night we slept like logs. The following day we helped him bring his cows home for milking with the assistance of his Welsh corgi dog and when Lizzie sent me to get some extra milk at tea time a few days later, Mr. Edwards showed me how to milk a cow. I can smell that cowshed yet!

In the hot weather we sometimes headed for the beach carrying a towel and wearing a swim suit under our clothes. One day when I had just learnt to swim I got out of my depth, panicked and began swallowing sea water. An old sailor who lived near the beach came to my rescue; since then I have never been enthusiastic about swimming but I still enjoyed playing with my friends in the sea and on the sand dunes. The quickest way to reach the dunes after swimming was by crossing the dock gates, which were in two sections allowing fishermen to open and shut them by moving each half to the side to let their boats in and out of the dock. These gates which formed a bridge of sorts were made of a number of planks of wood with large gaps between and a rope hand rail. We had all heard of a boy who had drowned by falling from the dock gates and I was terrified I would slip and fall in, so I preferred walking round the dock. My cousin Bobby remembers those lock gates too, and says he was just as frightened of falling in as I was; he too would rather walk round the dock. Now, they are long gone.

FUTURE STEPMOTHER

Dad came down to see us for the weekend that summer bringing with him an attractive young lady, called Anne. She was five feet seven and half inches tall with a good figure, wearing makeup and high heels; her auburn hair was piled up on the top of her head in the Edwardian manner. To us she looked like a film star and we had never met any one quite like her. Dad told us to call her 'Auntie'. I found out later that she was 26 years old.

On the Sunday morning Dad and 'Auntie' came to church with us all and instead of sitting in our usual seats on one side of the nave we sat in the centre. The organist always played the 'Trumpet Voluntary' whenever he saw Lizzie walking into church and he played it very emphatically on that particular Sunday morning. Afterwards I gave Lizzie my hat and she went home with Jim to cook dinner for us all while Terry and I, still wearing our best clothes, went down to the harbour with Dad and 'Auntie'. She was very pleasant, but I was upset to see my Dad arm in arm with her and felt very nervous about the future. Hearing him call her Anne and 'Darling' reminded me just how much I missed my mother whose name had also been Ann.

ANOTHER RETURN TO EDGWARE

A few weeks later Dad wrote to tell us that he wanted us to go back to live with him and 'Auntie' in Edgware. This did not go down at all well with me or Terry. We were happy enough where we were. I planned to leave school in a year's time and had begun to think about taking up a career in nursing.

Of course we had no choice in the matter and early one morning two of my friends, Maureen Rees and Millie Evans, came to Rhandir Delyn to say goodbye to me. I cried, cried and cried again. Neither Terry nor I wished to leave our friends or Lizzie and Jim, who must have been devastated, having given us a home and caring for us for several years. They would surely miss us a lot and I felt heart broken as we travelled on the train to London in the care of the guard. When we arrived at Paddington station I could see my Dad waiting for us at the barrier and he took us home to Edgware on the Underground train.

When we reached the house 'Auntie' was there to greet us. She had a kind face and a nice smile, but I was miserable. I didn't want anyone taking my mother's place. She and my Dad were very demonstrative in their feelings towards each other in front of Terry and me which hurt me and I could not understand why she called my father Michael. I thought it very strange for he was Bill or Willie to the rest of the family. All I wanted was to return to auntie Lizzie and my school friends in Wales.

My brother Terry and me.

Dad was still in the army, and went daily to the barracks in nearby Mill Hill. That first weekend he took us to a fair in nearby Chandos Park and we all went on the chairoplanes, which I liked, and instead of going to church on Sunday we all went to the cinema. The following day Terry and I attended school. It must have been very hard for 'Auntie' living in a house that our father had shared with our mother and dealing with me, a bolshie thirteen year old. I slept in my parents' former bedroom which constantly reminded me of my mother.

Getting to know and accept my stepmother took me a long time. Poor 'Auntie'. Terry was far more agreeable and adaptable than I was. She was always kind but not in the least motherly, though perhaps Terry would disagree with me about that, and she often placated my father when he lost his temper with me. She had been in the Land Army during the war and I remember once seeing her in a pair of jodhpurs which was an unusual sight for I had never seen anyone wearing them. She helped me with my handwriting which was appalling at that time and is not much better today!

Even though the war was over clothing coupons were required to buy clothes or material with which to make them. 'Auntie' was a tailoress so she was able to make her own clothes and always wore high heels. She was the manageress of a clothing firm in central London and every week from Monday to Friday she left home at 7am and did not return until evening. My father taught Terry and me how to lay the dinner table 'in the correct way' with a dessert fork, side plate and butter knife and how to prepare vegetables for dinner which 'Auntie' cooked when she returned home. He taught me how to make a pot of tea by taking the pot to the kettle

We all sat down to dinner at about 7pm while listening to a daily serial on the wireless, called 'Dick Barton Special Agent'. Terry and I were unaccustomed to buttering our own bread or eating a large meal so late in the day. It took some getting used to. Dad put up a rota on the kitchen door for us to take turns washing the dishes afterwards, before we were allowed out to play with our friends and at weekends they did the housework together, sometimes well into the night. Naturally we were expected to keep our bedrooms tidy.

I found my father very pedantic, domineering and completely unapproachable, and consequently I was very lonely. I seldom saw my friend Janet as she had learnt to ride a bicycle. But one day my father brought home a second hand bike for me and taught me how to ride it and after that my life became more bearable and Janet and I went off together on our bicycles after dinner or at weekends, which upset her mother at first, for fear we would get lost, but we never did.

Even though the war in Europe was over, life was still very austere and we were still at war with Japan. Food rationing was still in force and I missed Lizzie's cooking. We never ate any stewed fruit or apple pies any more and we all found it difficult to adjust to our new life, my father included. For now he had a lovely young companion with whom he wished to spend his time and in the evenings they often took themselves off to our local public house 'The Flying Eagle' where they could smoke and drink, leaving Terry and me at home alone.

I did not realise it at the time, but it was only because 'Auntie' earned good money in London that the household bills were paid and we had food on our table every day. Certainly there was never much of it in the larder. Many years later, our stepmother told me that Terry and I wrote to Lizzie and Addie, to complain that we had to do all the housework. After a very short time our father reflected on our situation and decided that we should return to Wales until he had been discharged from the army. So he took us to Paddington station together with my bicycle and put us on the train for Burry Port in the care of the guard.

CHAPTER FOURTEEN

Return to Burry Port

I have no recollection of exactly how Terry felt when we returned to Wales but I was extremely happy. Lizzie welcomed us back with open arms. She had such a sweet smile with rosy cheeks and was kindness itself, always doing someone a good turn. I think she must have loved us dearly. Jim too was very pleased to see us.

In just those few weeks Lizzie seemed to have shrunk. Terry and I were beginning to look down on her. On market day she enjoyed taking us on the bus to Llanelly, where she always bought a popular Welsh delicacy called laver bread, made from seaweed it was fried and eaten at breakfast time with bacon. Terry and I never liked it but our uncle Tom Bowen was ecstatic about it and in later years when he lived in London, if any one in the family went to Wales he would say 'Bring me back some laver bread.' I myself loved Lizzie's Welsh Rarebit and her Welsh cakes.

It was great to be back with my friends at school. Dad had given me a satchel to carry my homework and when weather permitted I cycled to school or came home on the crossbar of the bicycle of my classmate Raymond, travelling at speed downhill from Elkington to Colby Road. I adored the freedom of cycling with my girl friends, for the only traffic was an occasional farm cart or delivery van. A favourite place to visit was the Gower peninsula seen across the estuary from my bedroom window. It is a picturesque part of south Wales with quiet lanes, delightful villages, tiny churches and great sea views. I particularly remember visiting the village of Pen-clawdd to see the famous cockle women on the beach with their donkeys, and also the beautiful Rhossilli bay.

Much of the countryside of Carmarthenshire is pastoral and was very attractive and traffic free in the nineteen forties. I enjoyed cycling with my girl friends to Kidwelly castle and then on through quiet tree lined lanes to Ferry Side, with Llanstephan castle on the hill across the estuary. Sometimes we got as far as the county town of Carmarthen, fifteen miles from Burry Port. There we would stop on the bridge over the Towy to watch the coracle fishermen at work before eating our picnic. I loved the history of King Arthur and the Knights of the Round Table. It is said that Merlin was born in Carmarthen town and I always visited his rather bedraggled oak tree: I am told a remnant of it is kept in their Civic Hall now. I slept well after these excursions.

A friendly Mrs. Williams and her son ran a laundry service in West Wales and called at Lizzie's every week in a small van delivering clean laundry. In the school holidays for the past year or so we had enjoyed travelling round with one or other of them helping to deliver the laundry in our district and we willingly did so again whenever we could.

A NEW COUSIN

Aunt Addie came to Burry Port in August 1945 bringing me a pot of Paquins face cream, lavender perfume, a suspender belt and some nylon stockings with seams which were the height of fashion that she had bought with her clothing coupons. I wore them to Sunday morning communion at St Mary's together with a fashionable second hand suit which Lizzie had altered to fit me and a pair of her sandals with little heels which made me feel very sophisticated and grown up. Addie was much fatter than usual and sat with her feet up in the afternoons which was most unlike her. When I asked her why, she told me she was expecting a baby soon. Her son Robert, known to me as Bobby, was born in Neath that September about a month after the end of the second world war which was known as VJ Day (Victory over Japan) because we defeated the Japanese.

We did not know that on the 6th August 1945 America dropped an atomic bomb on the Japanese city of Hiroshima which completely devastated it but the Japanese refused to surrender until about four days later when America dropped a second atomic bomb on the city of Nagasaki. The destruction was so horrendous the Japanese were forced to capitulate..... at last the war was over. The result is that Japan leads the world in trying to prevent a catastrophe ever happening again, anywhere in the world.

Uncle Jim Marcroft was soon demobbed from the army and as he had been trained as a chef he was employed as a chef in an hotel in Crowborough in Sussex and Mary and little Michael joined him there, leaving Addie with baby Bobby in Cymmer looking after Gran Hill where I spent the half term and enjoyed taking Bobby for walks in his pram. He had bright red curly hair and looked absolutely gorgeous in knitted suits of yellow or apple green. He was a complete bundle of energy, never still, just like his father.

CYMRU GROES

Lizzie now allowed me to stay out until 9 30pm. on Friday nights so that I could join the church youth club called 'Cymru Groes'. What fun we had. It was there I discovered the real attraction of the opposite sex when playing Postman's Knock and other great 'kissing games'. All so innocent, too! Because it had no street lights Cwm Ifor Road was a favourite haunt for courting couples at night and at dusk it was full of hateful bats so when I returned from the club Lizzie and Jim suggested I call out like Tarzan to let them know I was coming up the lane. They would then come out of their front door to meet me and I would run up as fast as my legs would carry me.

I still dream about Lizzie sometimes. As a young girl she wanted to be a missionary in China but family responsibility and her weak health made it impossible. She was what can only be described as a good woman for I never heard her speak ill of any one. She was very religious in a nice way and made us conscious of God's presence in our daily lives. She regularly visited the sick of the parish and when she was not cleaning the house or working in her large garden she would busy baking and making fruit preserves most of which if not eaten by us or her family she either gave to the needy or it was sold in church bazaars. She was also an accomplished needle woman but I never saw her knitting or reading a book. She encouraged me to help her make soft toys for my little cousins at Christmas time and for one so small, with only one kidney, she moved with remarkable energy.

FREDERICK HANDEL

One day there was a film about Frederick Handel at our local cinema in Burry Port and despite her poor eye sight and weak bladder Lizzie came with me to see it because she loved his music. She had a good singing voice and enjoyed singing hymns in church and although I was tone deaf, I liked singing hymns too and joined my school choir.

To celebrate the end of the war our choir combined with a local male voice choir in a Burry Port chapel to sing Welsh hymns and the Hallelujah Chorus from Handel's Messiah. It was a very uplifting experience, for the acoustics in the chapel were marvellous and after the performance I realised just why Lizzie liked Handel's music so much. In the eighteenth century when George ll attended the first performance of The Messiah in Covent Garden, he was so impressed with the Hallelujah Chorus that he rose to his feet and remained standing to the end, thus forcing the whole assembly to do likewise. He established a tradition that night, and ever since audiences always stand when it is performed live, as we did that night at the Burry Port chapel.

I have never had the opportunity to take David to a chapel in Wales to hear a male voice choir singing hymns in Welsh, but one day we attended a concert given by the London Welsh Choir in a Surrey village hall. That evening the whole audience including ourselves joined in singing our favourite hymn 'How Great Thou Art'. We found it was truly memorable and a very uplifting experience

When our son Malcolm was at university David's mother often stayed with us at weekends and one Sunday evening she was present when we were watching hymn singing on TV and as usual I joined in. Suddenly she turned to me and said 'Kathy, I wish you wouldn't do that: you can't sing!' David was furious with her, and told her off, saying he always enjoyed listening to me singing hymns. But she was right, I cannot sing, and naturally I forgave her.

TRADITIONAL FESTIVITIES

On 31st October 1945 we held our first Halloween party at Rhandir Delyn. Lizzie produced a couple of large turnips holding lighted candles and she put some delicious eating apples from the orchard in a large pail of water for us to play 'apple bobbing' on the kitchen floor followed by Hide and Seek and 'Sardines' inside the house. There was no 'Trick or Treat' when we were children or when our son Malcolm was a boy. That idea has come from the United States in the late twentieth century.

Lizzie and Jim celebrated their twentieth wedding anniversary on the 5th of November 1945 and we were told at school that three hundred and forty years ago to the day, Guy Fawkes was the traitor who tried to blow up the Houses of Parliament and King James VI and I with gunpowder and that all over Great Britain it was a tradition on that day to burn Guy Fawkes effigy on a bonfire. For the first time since the war ended everyone could celebrate the occasion by doing just that very thing. We made a guy dressed in Jim's old clothes and placed it on the top of a large bonfire in the garden and invited our friends to join us. We ate potatoes baked in the fire and lit many sparklers. It was very enjoyable.

At Christmas time Lizzie took us to see a matinee performance of the pantomime Cinderella in the Swansea Empire and when the actor playing Buttons called me up on to the stage I was overcome with shyness. On the way back to Swansea station we joined a large queue at a greengrocer's shop where bananas and peaches were on sale for the first time since the war began. I loved the bananas but I was very disappointed with the peaches and I still am today!

During my school years I do not recall hearing what I now consider tasteless jokes or bad language except for an occasional outburst of blasphemy and neither I nor any of my girl friends ever smoked cigarettes. It was not the fashion then and we had no money. I think some of the boys smoked cigarettes behind the cycle shed at school! I never ever saw anybody spit because the penalty for spitting was five pounds, which was a lot of money then. I wish there was a penalty for spitting today. I hate to see sportsmen doing it. Neither did I or any of our friends ever play in our bedrooms; when I was young bedrooms were used only to sleep in, and friends came to tea only on birthdays or when specially invited, possibly because of food rationing. Of course, children had much more freedom to play with their friends in the open air, even in cold weather, for there was no traffic on the streets and there never seemed to be any restrictions, as long as we were home for meals and by bed time. It was a very different world from the one we live in today.

Although Christmas celebrations during the second world war were muted because families were separated and food was rationed, we children always gave and received presents. Every year Lizzie made a Christmas pudding containing silver threepenny pieces and charms. Terry and I, and Janet too when she was with us, following a long tradition, gave the mixture a stir with a wooden spoon and made a wish before it was placed in a pudding basin and cooked and stored until Christmas Day, when it was heated up and eaten with custard, and we were thrilled if we found a silver threepenny bit. Until I was thirteen years old we all went to church on Christmas morning, but when I had been confirmed Lizzie let me attend midnight mass on Christmas Eve with my friends instead. Afterwards we sang carols all the way home.

On New Year's morning during the second world war it was

a popular custom in Burry Port for children to get up early to sing carols outside neighbours' front doors while they were still in bed. We enjoyed doing it and the favourite carols for the New Year were 'God Rest You Merry Gentlemen' and wassail songs such as 'Here We Come a Wassailing Among the Leaves so Green'. Our neighbours responded cheerfully, always getting out of bed to greet us. There was no television to keep people up very late and a dark haired boy at the door on New Year's morning was considered lucky so Terry, whose hair had become dark, led the way and we were made welcome and given money for sweets wherever we went. When I met David I found that in Scotland there is a tradition called 'First Footing' at New Year, when just after midnight on New Year's Day a dark haired man carrying food and drink and crossing the threshold of a house brings luck to everyone inside. Scots whiskey and shortbread is usual.

I was in Cymmer when Tom came home on leave from the Fleet Air Arm and saw his baby son for the first time. He was so delighted he went potty! He took Bobby in his arms and did the sailors' hornpipe all round the living room and up on to the dining table with Addie following him, laughing, but begging him to stop! It was a very happy time. He brought them presents from America. There was a pair of pretty shoes with wedge heels for Addie which I thought were sensational (I was becoming fashion conscious) and for his baby son he brought a black toy dog. Years later when Bobby had grown up and David and I with our small son Malcolm were on a visit to Addie and Tom in Ealing, Addie gave the toy dog to Malcolm and when he left to go to university David had it sitting on the window sill in his darkroom for a long time.

In Burry Port after the second world war, a ghastly power station was built down by the sea shore where we used to swim, and it obliterated the view of the estuary from Rhandir Delyn. I am pleased to say it has long since been demolished and replaced in 2000 by a pleasant Estuary Walk and Cycle Way from the Gower through Llanelli and Burry Port to the nearby village of Pembrey. Burry Port dock is now an attractive boating marina and the view of the estuary from the house has been restored.

SCHOOL FRIENDS

In my last year at school I spent a lot of time with my friend Maureen and my bike became extremely useful because she lived near Pembrey. Maureen liked one particular boy in our class called Tony. His best friend was Raymond on whose bicycle crossbar I sometimes rode home from school. At weekends after church the four of us would go for walks in the country lanes or down by the Burry Port Dock and steal an innocent kiss or two.

In the Spring of 1946 when I was fourteen I spent a holiday in Cymmer with Addie, baby Bobby and Gran. I helped look after Bobby. Addie and I painted the kitchen and washed blankets by hand and wrung them out over the sink! Then we climbed up the mountainside, to hang them on the clothes line. There were still two or three hens at the very top of the garden left there by Ron Smith, and they had to be fed each day. I liked going to see if they had laid any eggs.

Terry and I had begun to accept the fact that we would be returning to Edgware to live with my Dad and auntie Anne, and I began seriously thinking about my future career. I knew I had always enjoyed looking after my little cousins during school holidays, so I decided I would tell my father I would like to become a children's nurse. I realised I would have to wait two years or more before I could take up training. Returning to London as we did, I had the consolation of knowing that I would see Winnie and Arthur and their children in Colindale and Bill and Kitty and their son Terry in Twickenham. One day, Addie told me she and Tom and Bobby would come to live in London. Little did either of us realise that she would remain in Cymmer with Bobby, looking after Gran Hill for almost four years.

Reluctantly, in August 1946 Terry and I said goodbye to Lizzie, Jim and our school friends and together with my bicycle, we boarded the train for Paddington in the care of the Guard. My school days were over.

CHAPTER FIFTEEN

Growing Up

In 1946 we returned to live in Edgware, with Dad and our new Auntie. Dad had been been demobbed from the army and was working as a painter and decorator again and travelling to work on a bicycle; Auntie was manageress of a clothing factory in central London. Terry returned to school and at first I stayed at home, doing the household chores every morning and preparing vegetables for dinner, until arrangements could be made for my temporary employment prior to a nursing career. My spirits were very low and I longed to return to Wales. There were no books at home except paper backs by Zane Gray, detective stories and a tattered volume of The Ragged Trousered Philanthropist. So to cheer myself I read the Daily Mirror every day and enjoyed the cartoons 'Garth' and 'Jane' and the 'Old Codgers' Live Letters column.

Auntie had good strong legs and rode a Raleigh cycle with a crossbar and toe clips which she kept in our garage; she was born in Nottingham where Raleigh bikes were manufactured. She loved ballroom dancing too, and at dinner one evening she persuaded Dad to go to dancing classes with her at our local school, leaving us alone at home. Afterwards they called in at the Flying Eagle public house in Mollison Way to enjoy a glass of beer and smoke cigarettes, remaining there until closing time at 10.30pm. She was the first woman I ever saw smoking a cigarette and for several years they both tried unsuccessfully to give up the habit. Eventually Dad rolled his own tobacco which he kept in a pouch.

My friend Janet introduced me to Radio Luxembourg, which played popular records, and Dad connected our wireless to an aerial in our loft to pick up the signal so that when he and Auntie were out I tuned in with the volume right up. Many times I tried to talk to him about my mother but somehow the words always stuck in my throat.

The second world war was over, but food and clothes were still rationed and as winter approached the weather turned bitterly cold. There was a great shortage of coal throughout the country and, as almost every home had coal fires and power stations were fuelled by coal as well, it was a great problem for industry and the recently elected Labour Government was forced to introduce power cuts every day. Heavy snow in January and February 1947 exacerbated the situation. At home we possessed two small electric fires and just enough coal for Dad to light a fire every evening. He bought us second hand winter coats and Terry was sent back to school in Wales for a while. Auntie made me a warm figure-hugging step-in house coat with a zip up the front out of a grey army blanket; we both wore thick lisle stockings with seams up the back of the leg. When they laddered she taught me how to darn them, because we had no coupons to buy more.

The cinema was the main source of entertainment for the populace in the immediate post-war years. There were four of these large art deco buildings within walking distance of our home, the Odeon, the Rialto, the Adelphi and the Savoy. They all had comfortable seats showing American and British films and they were great places to keep warm: some cinemas even had a tea room in the foyer and all showed two films plus a newsreel twice a day on a large screen. It was a magical world to me and while films were in progress uniformed usherettes with the aid of torches showed customers to their seats in the dark auditoriums and came round selling ice-cream in cartons. During intervals dim lights were switched on and some cinemas had an electric organ playing while the usherettes sold ice cream at the foot of the aisles. Cigarette smoking was permitted everywhere at all times and ash trays were attached to the back of every other seat. In that freezing winter with daily power cuts and a lack of coal we went to the cinema every Saturday and Sunday afternoon to keep warm. My favourite cinema was The Savoy in Burnt Oak where the carpet was so thick we bounced as we walked in. I began to buy Picturegoer magazine and sent away for autographed photos of American film stars. My favourite was Tyrone Power.

In January 1947 Dad sent me to the Labour Exchange and I got a job as a filing clerk in a modern factory in Queensbury. I hated it so much I stayed there just two weeks. On a bitterly cold winter day that month the Exchange sent me to another job at a factory in Colindale where I bottled men's hair cream, called 'Nufix'. I have no idea what possessed me to work there. It was a dreadful place where the vast majority of employees were women who used bad language and made ribald remarks about Princess Elizabeth and her future husband. I stayed there for four weeks, during which time there were many heavy snow falls.

To help pay the mortgage during the time I worked there Dad let my bedroom to a young married couple, Mr and Mrs Crane. For a few weeks I slept in Terry's room. Dad disliked Mr Crane because he was too familiar with me and called me 'Kathy' instead of Kathleen. He frequently told him not to do so. Mrs Crane was heavily pregnant and after three weeks she was taken by ambulance in a snow storm to Edgware General Hospital where her baby was born. Ten days later she returned home with her baby.

One icy morning a few days later when Mr Crane had left for work she decided to wash her baby in a bathtub beside the small electric fire in their bed sitting room. It was extremely cold yet she was wearing only a silk dressing gown tied with a knotted cord. I was about to leave home for work myself, when I heard the most awful scream from above and ran to the foot of our stairs to see Mrs Crane standing with Dad on our landing: her dressing gown was alight and he was trying to remove it. On a rare day off work, Auntie emerged from their bedroom with a rug and between them she and Dad pushed Mrs Crane to our landing floor and rolled her in the rug, putting out the flames.

My last glimpse of the poor woman, before I fled down to our sitting room and dialled 999 on our recently installed telephone, was of her sitting on the carpet in their room, wearing what re-mained of her corselette. Then I left for work. A couple of weeks later she died of septicaemia in Edgware General Hospital and their little baby was adopted, which was very sad. After such a traumatic event Dad always became angry if he saw me wearing a dressing gown with a knotted cord; he was also paranoid about the possibility of a house fire. If I returned home after he had retired to bed he always got up to check that I had switched off the electricity. There was no such thing as a smoke alarm in those days.

Some time during this awful winter Dad's uncle Will was cross-ing a road in Euston when he was knocked down and killed by a taxi. Dad, Auntie, and Winnie and Arthur all went to his funeral and his aunt Sue was there from Sarn and she told my Dad to take care of Terry and me.

One happy memory of that winter was that once a week we would settle down in the dark, round the coal fire in the dining room, to listen to a good murder mystery on the wireless called Appointment with Fear. Valentine Dyall, an actor with a very spooky voice, always introduced it, saying 'This is your story teller .... the Man in Black.' Just at the most frightening part of the story my Dad would deliberately let out a wail like a banshee, which always made me jump out of my skin.

Auntie suggested that I and my new friend Sybil, who lived nearby, join the beginners ballroom dancing class at the school. There we learnt the waltz, quickstep and fox-trot, and old time dances called the Military Two Step, the Gay Gordons and the St Bernard's Waltz, all of which were lots of fun and kept us warm. In the early spring of 1947 Auntie's brother Ron, a soldier several years her senior, came to stay with us for a few days. I liked him and Dad invited him to join us at a dance at the school. He was very handsome in his army dress uniform and could dance and I enjoyed myself a lot. From that night Auntie and I began to get to know each other a little better and I was pleased that Terry had come home from Burry Port.

I often visited Winnie at weekends, finding her washing clothes on Saturday afternoons in one of the first washing machines I ever saw. Like her father and my Dad, Winnie had a highly developed interest in politics and was a staunch supporter of the Labour Party. When she was a girl her father had held occasional party meetings at home in Aberkenfig. In adult life she expressed a keen interest in education and loved to debate the issues of the day. She thoroughly enjoyed a good argument and had a ready wit. She was our son

Malcolm's favourite great aunt. Her husband Arthur had a quiet sense of humour. He was an excellent carpenter, obvious from the handmade furniture in their home. Their kitchen was full of fitted cupboards long before the fashion and they had a refrigerator fitted in and a speaker relaying the wireless programmes from their sitting room so that Winnie could listen while she worked - all extremely modern at the time. But like everyone else as yet, their home was heated by coal fires.

CHAPTER SIXTEEN

Dressmaking

That spring of 1947 clothing coupons ceased and the New Look fashion appeared with longer skirts, wasp waists and high heels. Auntie made herself some highly fashionable clothes and instead of working in the city of London she started a dressmaking business at home which began to thrive. She made herself outfits in the latest fashion and wore black suede court shoes with very high heels. She made me some dresses too and people sometimes mistook us for sisters when we were out shopping. She was kind and took care of Terry and me when we were unwell.

Dad suggested I should try my hand at dressmaking too; after all at Lizzie's I had learnt embroidery. If I turned out to be as good at needlework, he said, we could make it a family business.

So through contacts he found me a position in a small dressmaking firm in Edgware, within walking distance of home. Everyone working there was very kind to me including the manager and I learnt how to sew on buttons and press studs but little else except how to make tea. I hated it and my hands were always perspiring. Thankfully, after only one month the manager wrote to my father, and said 'We all love Kathleen, she is a delightful girl, but please take her away.........she is useless at dressmaking!'

SPEEDWAY

I was fifteen years old, wearing makeup and high heels, and my next job was on the sweets and biscuits counter at Woolworth's in Colindale. There I made a friend called Josie who introduced me to speedway racing at Wembley Stadium. Every Thursday evening from late April to October 1947 I travelled on my own to the stadium from Queensbury tube station; there I met Josie and two boy friends, and shouted myself hoarse for the 'Wembley Lions', especially Captain Bill Kitchen, Split Waterman and Bronco Wilson.

Afterwards we travelled home together by bus; at the end of the journey I always had a good ten minute walk alone, arriving home at 10pm. One night, Josie and I missed the last bus which meant a three mile walk from Wembley Stadium: our boy friends were good enough to walk with us all the way, so that when I reached my house, well after midnight, I was not unduly perturbed at the late hour, but my father was extremely angry. At the time I could not understand why! Next morning even though my feet were very sore from walking all that way in high heels my father insisted I got up and went to work.

My friend Sybil asked me make up a foursome and go to a dance on a blind date with her and her boy friend at the Frigidaire Company where Mr Smith a friendly neighbour worked. My Dad gave me permission to go because Mr Smith agreed to bring us home in his car. My 'blind date' called Peter was nice looking and pleasant: he could dance and I enjoyed the evening. Much to my surprise a couple of days later he called at my home in his car. I was most impressed until he told me that he and his family were emigrating to Canada. I never heard from him again. Shortly afterwards Sybil also emigrated to Canada, to live with her mother and new stepfather.

The summer of 1947 was the hottest for many years and we all wore very little clothing at weekends and tar macadam bubbled on the road surfaces. One Saturday morning I was first up, to find our kitchen had been invaded by ants. They had found the sugar and the frame of the hall doorway was covered with thousands of them. Dad called the environmental health officer from the local council and he surrounded our house with DDT powder and took a blow torch to a large ants' nest in our garden (DDT is now banned as an insecticide). Dad had no qualms about killing the ants, but he never killed a spider. He said it was unlucky and always picked them up and put them in the garden. David won't kill them either: he says they help keep the nasty creepy crawlies out of our home.

We wanted a dog and persuaded Dad to buy a crossbred terrier pup which we called Bob. Auntie looked after him because she was working at home. He was a friendly little mongrel and would be up at the sitting room window watching for us all to come home.

Terry went on holiday to Devon with Dad and Auntie that summer, and I stayed with auntie Winnie and our little dog went into kennels. When Dad returned from Devon they found Bob was very ill with canine distemper and he died, which saddened us all.

I still have a guilty conscience when I recall the day I agreed to take Terry to see Wembley Lions Speedway. We set out for Queensbury tube station but when we got there I did not have enough money to pay for him, so I sent him home. How could I have done that? It was a dreadful thing to do. I should have stayed at home too.

This was a period of my life when I was self-centred and generally found my father difficult to live with. His temper was explosive and he was very domineering. I did not realise that he had financial problems and had renewed the mortgage on our house. He insisted I help in the home before going out to enjoy myself, which was only right, but I did not like his attitude at all. I loathed Sundays: I seemed to have nothing interesting to do except cooking and housework late into the night, after which I lay in bed reading detective stories until the early hours. Occasionally when I was out in the evenings my Dad came looking for me in the street, in high dudgeon. I could not understand why he always expected me home at a certain time. There was no such thing as mobile phones, but I did begin to like Auntie who sometimes interceded on my behalf.

One morning that hot summer, when we were all at home, she responded to a knock on our front door and was confronted by a black travelling salesman. At sight of him she screamed, 'Michael!' My Dad came running! Neither Auntie, Terry nor I had ever seen a black man. How times have changed!

MENDIP HILLS

Ever since our mother had died Terry and I had attended a chest clinic twice a year for x-rays: in the autumn of 1947 I had little appetite and began to lose weight, I tired quickly and suffered from night sweats. An x-ray showed I had a shadow on my lung which meant I had tuberculosis. Shock horror! Dad wrote to a sanatorium run by Anglican nuns in the Mendip Hills, begging them to take me as a patient. They agreed and in late October he and Auntie took me there by train; on our arrival the nursing nuns were surprised because I looked so well. His letter had given them the impression that I was dying.

The sanatorium had male and female patients and for six months I slept on the first floor in an open air balcony with five other young women in their teens. We enjoyed a splendid view of Glastonbury Tor and lived on a diet of good food, fresh air and bed rest, as my mother had done when she was in Craig yr Nos. I believe it was still the only treatment for tuberculosis.

I spent the first three months in bed, except to wash and go to the loo. I was in bed the day that Princess Elizabeth married Prince Philip in November 1947 and one cold night that December I woke to see a tawny owl sitting on the end of my bed.

I put on about two stone in weight and in January I was allowed to get up and dress and attend the chapel there, where male and female patients were segregated by the aisle. A few days later I walked in the grounds and in the early spring of 1948 I was allowed to walk with other inmates through country lanes and fields of anemones which reminded me of my beloved mother. The clear air and good food did wonders for me and I was soon strong enough to visit Axbridge village, have coffee and do shopping for the less fortunate patients. It was wonderful to feel well and the Somerset countryside was simply beautiful.

Just before Easter the doctor said I was fit enough to go home. My Dad came to fetch me in a hired car and he and Auntie stayed three nights at the Lamb Hotel in Axbridge and took me out on day trips. Good Friday was my 16th birthday and the temperature was unusually high at 90°F. We visited the attractive little village of Cheddar and the famous caves full of stalagmites and stalactites which were beautifully lit and awe inspiring. Next day we motored to the top of Cheddar Gorge and drank cider in an ancient public house. Then on Easter Sunday I said goodbye to the nuns and the other patients and we drove home through the spring countryside of the south of England. There was very little traffic, because few people had cars, and I loved it all.

When I arrived home I discovered that Terry was away in a sanatorium and many years later Anne told she never had any children of her own because it was too dangerous to contemplate having a baby when both of us were ill with tuberculosis.

The Labour government introduced the National Health Service that year which entitled everyone to free medical, optical and dental treatment. Dad took Terry and me to the dentist for the first time since primary school and he had some dentures made. On the way home he told me he was sure that the book The Ragged Trousered Philanthropists had instigated the politicians to introduce the NHS.

That year Addie came on a brief visit to Edgware with Bobby. They stayed with the Dixon family and while Addie was talking with Janet's mother, Flo, little Bobbie opened a cupboard, found a tin of golden syrup and poured it into a box of corn flakes!!! Like my brother he was a little devil!

Janet Dixon and I seldom saw each other any more as we had little in common for she had a different set of friends but she did invite me in to listen to two records on her new wind-up record player, one of someone called Frank Sinatra and the other of a group called 'The Inkspots'. She thought Frank Sinatra was wonderful, but it took several more years for me to become enraptured!

When Terry came home from the sanatorium Dad and Auntie often invited friends in to play whist and cribbage and we joined in when they played table skittles. I had no close friends and whenever I could I escaped in red shorts on my old bicycle. That summer I visited Bill and Kitty and cousin Terry in Twickenham. Terry was very shy and hid behind Kitty's skirts all the time I was there. Sadly, Dinda their lovely old springer spaniel had gone to his doggie heaven but Bill aged thirty two was still extremely handsome and blessed with a wonderful singing voice, a bit like Bing Crosby's. While I was there he took a microphone linked to their wireless set and disappeared into another room and sang a romantic song to me. I thought he was superb. It was a hot day and he took me to a neighbour's flat to get a cold drink and it was the first time I had a drink with ice cubes.

WELSH HOLIDAY

A few days later Dad put me on the train, with my bicycle sporting a red and white Wembley Lions speedway pennant, to stay with Lizzie and Jim for two weeks' holiday in Wales. I had fun visiting all my old school friends who were amazed to learn that in London, cinemas and public houses were open on Sundays and were astounded when I told them I often went to the cinema instead of going to church.

Addie had given me a pretty off the shoulder summer dress to wear and Auntie had made me a lovely blue dirndl skirt with which I wore a Hungarian blouse, all the height of fashion. One morning while I was walking down Church Hill in high heels to visit Granny Bowen and Muriel I met one of Lizzie's friends and she could not believe I was only sixteen.

My friend Maureen dared me to go out with a good looking charming young man who was a newcomer to Burry Port and enjoyed cycling. Foolishly, without really knowing him, I took up the challenge and on a beautiful sunny day we went for a cycle ride to the village of Pembrey. We ended up on the local golf course.

When it began to rain we took shelter under a corrugated awning. There it was that, for a few minutes, I almost had a fate worse than death. I was innocent and completely unreceptive, and his ardour quickly cooled!! I learnt a lesson that day and I was very glad to get back to the safety of Rhandir Delyn. I found out later that he was aged twenty one: much too old!

My friend Barbara, who lived in The Garden Suburb, knew some of the Llanelly football players, and one Saturday afternoon we travelled with three of them on the train from Burry Port to watch them play Swansea. After that I became a Llanelly fan.

A couple of days later I took the train up the Afan valley to see Addie, little Bobby and Gran Hill in Cymmer and Emily and family in Abergwynfi, with whom I spent Derby Day. Va backed the winner, 'My Love', which delighted us all. Next day I took the train to Bridgend and a bus to Aberkenfig and walked up Sarn Hill to stay with great aunt Sue. It was lovely to see her. She was now a widow and all her sons had left home. Auntie Bessie and her family lived nearby and I had fun with my cousins Betty and Keith and met Bessie's youngest daughter, two year old Jennifer. On my return to Burry Port Jim came home from work and lay down on the settee in the dining room and fell asleep. After a few minutes he began to make a strange noise, and started to foam at the mouth. I told Lizzie I was sure he was having a fit. A few minutes later, totally confused, he sat up and began to put on his shoes and make as if he was about to go to work. Two days later I said goodbye to them and put my bike in the guard's van on the train to Paddington where Dad met me. The next time I saw Addie she told me that Jim was having treatment for epilepsy.

My relationship with my father at this time was extremely difficult having gone from bad to worse. I wanted freedom to come and go at will and he would not allow me to make any decisions for myself. His temper was volcanic. I was extremely rebellious and I even thought about leaving home. One day I told him I had a brain of my own and could decide what I wanted to do to which he replied 'I am your brain and I tell you what to do!' He raised his hand to strike me and Auntie came between us and defended my corner and somehow we got through a very tense six months which I thought was caused by my desire to return to Wales, but perhaps it was just growing pains. Now when I hear of parents having trouble with their teenagers I smile. Little did I think it would ever happen to us with our dear son Malcolm, for we had a very stable and loving relationship with him until he was sixteen. Then one day almost overnight he rebelled and sadly we have never been as close as before which grieves us deeply.

Dad told us that a very famous person would visit us on Christmas Day 1948. That morning we were still in bed when we heard Bing Crosby's voice singing White Christmas. He was the famous person! Dad's present to us all was an electric record player, and a pile of new 78 records including Rosemary Clooney singing Kind Hearts and Gentle People and others!!! What a thrill it was. Truly. After Christmas dinner, we all had a great time listening to those records. On Boxing Day Auntie and I prepared food for a party of their friends and dressed up. Dad installed a barrel of beer and rolled back the carpet in the dining room and we danced well into the night to music on our new record player.

Terry looked very tired when he got up next day and two days later we had another party until the early hours. Looking back it was foolish of us to stay up so late. He was good looking, growing up fast and dating the girls. He spent ages in the bathroom which was most uncharacteristic. He had a good singing voice and knew all the popular songs played on the wireless every day.

I had become aware that my father and Anne, as I was now beginning to call her, were not married. I decided to accept the situation but said nothing to Terry. I believe the reason was that she was already married and had to wait seven years for a divorce, which was the law then.

CHAPTER SEVENTEEN

Beginning a Nursing Career

As I approached the age of seventeen, Dad had been making enquiries about my becoming a nurse at a local hospital where most of the patients were children. All I had to do was pass the entrance exam, which I did with flying colours, and I was offered a two year training course. To celebrate Dad took me out and bought me a fashionable herringbone tweed suit with a flared skirt and fitted jacket and Anne bought me some nice lingerie, including three pairs of cami-knickers which I loved wearing.

For a few weeks I worked at a shoe shop and then at Stanley Lee's, a small department store opposite Edgware station. In April 1949, wearing my new suit, I entered the gates of the Royal National Orthopaedic Hospital on the top of Brockley Hill, Stanmore, in Middlesex, as a trainee student nurse with eleven other novices between 17 and 18 years of age. We were taken to a large Victorian house within the hospital grounds which became our home and school for eight weeks and we had to be in bed with lights out at 11pm every night.

This hospital was affiliated to five London teaching hospitals so that when we qualified in Orthopaedics we could go on to do a short General Registration at one of them and I put my name down for University College Hospital in Euston.

Our uniform was a white dress and a cap in a butterfly shape; we provided our own flat black lace up shoes and black nylon stockings with seams; tights did not exist. Jewellery was forbidden and makeup was discouraged. We ate in the hospital dining room and our weekends were free.

My fellow students were well educated pleasant girls, a few of whom had been to boarding school. Some of us became friends and with the passing years I very much regret losing touch with six of them. There was my room mate Isobel, known as Dizzie, who was a madcap only child, prone to hysterical laughter at the least provocation. She had been to finishing school in Switzerland and had beautiful clothes. Her parents were wealthy, but separated. Her mother lived in an exclusive area off Park Lane, useful as a base when we were off duty.

Dorothy, known as Dossie, was an amusing Welsh girl, full of the devil and a great tease, with whom I was very compatible; we became firm friends. Joy, an attractive, sensitive girl a year older than me was a born nurse: she became my greatest friend and we planned to do our state registration together at University College Hospital. I was a frequent visitor at her home in Bushey and her parents and young sister were delightful. Eventually she married Bob Anderson who trained as a doctor at University College Medical School and became an orthopaedic surgeon.

Rowena, who had the most unusual eyes, was the eldest of three children. Her father owned the village grocer's store at Abridge in Essex. She left nursing at the RNO because she could not stand the bedpan round! However, she changed her mind the following year and returned to do her SRN - State Registered Nurse - at St Bartholomew's hospital and later joined the Queen Alexandra's Royal Army Nursing Corps. We enjoyed each other's company until the day she was transferred to Hong Kong, where she met an army officer and got married.

Gillian, who wished to become a physiotherapist, came from Harrow, nearer to my home in Edgware than all the rest of our group of trainees. I sometimes spent a weekend there, finding myself tremendously impressed because it had a breakfast room, which I had never seen before. One weekend we went Scottish dancing with her friends in Harrow and shortly afterwards, early one morning, I was standing looking out of her bedroom window and she pointed to an athlete running round the local playing field and said 'That's Roger whom we met at Scottish dancing.' It meant nothing to me at the time but a few years later in May 1954 I discovered he was none other than Roger Bannister who was the first man to run a four minute mile. Gillian gave up orthopaedic nursing because she had a back injury and sadly we lost touch.

Ruth, a tall girl who wore spectacles and came from Northampton, brought her bicycle with her to the RNO and we two enjoyed cycling round the locality together. She went on to do her SRN at the Ratcliffe Infirmary in Oxford.

Aileen, a small redheaded Yorkshire lass, seemed totally dedicated to her career and even then we all thought she would probably continue nursing all her life. We imagined her becoming a Matron one day! I wonder if she did! With the passing years I very much regret losing touch with all of them except Joy with whom I kept in touch for many years even though she and her family went to live in New Zealand.

During the first few weeks we were tutored in nursing, anatomy, physiology and hygiene, especially concentrating on cleanliness when dealing with patients and dressings, making sure we knew how to scrub our hands clean before and afterwards, with practical lessons in bed making and the taking of temperatures; we learnt how to give injections by impregnating oranges with a syringe, and were instructed to pay attention to our grooming and finger nails. We were told never to run on the wards except for fire, haemorrhage or sister's tea. We passed our preliminary exams and tension relaxed when we became fully fledged orthopaedic student nurses.

Matron threw a hospital dance for us in another large house in the grounds of the hospital and Dad treated me to a pretty off the shoulder cotton dress with a drawstring neck which I thought was absolutely beautiful. We danced until almost midnight with young men we had never met before, and enjoyed every minute, walking back through the hospital grounds to our residence. The following day we were measured for student nurse uniforms before going on a week's leave in June.

MARGATE

Auntie Mary and uncle Jim Marcroft had just bought a four bedroom boarding house in Eton Road, Margate, ten minutes walk from the sea and they invited me to spend my holiday with them and their children Michael and Clive. I was their first and only guest that week. In those days Margate was a pleasant seaside resort and before breakfast each morning I got up early and walked along the promenade. Clive, a quiet little three year old, stayed beside Mary all day long. Michael aged seven wore glasses like my brother Terry's and I took him to school every morning.

Anne had made me some new clothes to wear and on the Saturday night I dressed up and went to Dreamland Ballroom alone and stood as all the girls did at the edge of the dance floor until a boy invited me to dance. I did not have to wait long! I had many partners and the evening passed quickly, finishing at 11pm with what was known in those days as the Last Waltz. By then my dancing partner was one of a group of sailors on weekend leave from their ship moored off Margate. Afterwards, my partner and I strolled along the sea front together.

The following afternoon I walked with him along the cliff top to Palm Bay and got sunburnt while listening to the band of the Royal Air Force and he pointed out his ship, moored in the channel. He sailed away that night. I have no idea where or why. I was really only interested in dancing!

I thoroughly enjoyed my stay in Margate and Mary began to call me 'Duchess' because she said I had begun to put on airs and graces! Perhaps it was because I was mixing with girls who had had a better education than I had had.

ROYAL NATIONAL ORTHOPAEDIC HOSPITAL

On our return to the RNO as new student nurses we moved to single rooms in the Nurses Home and were let loose on the wards for the first time in our uniform, a blue and white striped dress, starched white cap and apron with a bib. We also had an attractive navy cape with a red lining and best of all, a navy blue double breasted belted outdoor coat with epaulets and brass buttons, and a jaunty peaked cap with an RNO badge on the front. So attractive and eye catching were they that when we were in London we were frequently mistaken for air hostesses.

We received free board and lodging and a salary of eight pounds a month, in cash. This was our spending money from which we bought our black shoes and stockings. At first I worked on a twenty bedded children's ward; most of the patients were in plaster casts for congenital dislocated hips. First year students did all the ward cleaning and on day one after giving the children breakfast I was nervous and looked lost, not knowing where to begin. A three year old whose name was Wendy virtually told me what to do, just like a kind old lady. She said 'Nurse! help make the beds and pull them all out to the middle, wipe the walls with a damp cloth and sprinkle the floor with wet tea leaves and sweep it; dust the cupboards and bring out the flowers from the side room.' In those days flowers were removed from wards at night because it was thought they absorbed too much oxygen. Afterwards Wendy asked me to stand her up to look out of the window. She loved that, and despite wearing a plaster cast she felt as light as a feather. So every morning, I lifted her up.

A consultant or senior doctor visited the ward every week. Sister knew when to expect him and nursing staff lined up in rank at the door, waiting with hands neatly clasped, and after she had greeted him we followed them round in silence. No one spoke to him except the ward sister. Consultants were treated like gods and sometimes acted like them too. That was how it was in the first years of the NHS. However, from my personal experience, more than fifty years later, as a patient in London teaching hospitals, that deference has all but disappeared. Whether or not it is a good thing I cannot judge.

My first experience of theatre was when I accompanied a girl of eleven for an operation on her Achilles tendon. I held the girl's hand while she was anaesthetised and then donned a cap and gown over my uniform, white wellies and a mask and scrubbed my hands with soap and running water for ten minutes as did the sur-

Lizzie and Jim Ogborn with Terry and me in Raeburn Road back garden.

geon and theatre staff, in a temperature of 90 degrees Fahrenheit. Then I stood and watched the surgeon take a scalpel and make the initial incision, like splitting an orange, which made me feel faint and momentarily I had to leave the theatre. Ever after I averted my eyes at the start of an operation. On average we stayed on a ward for six weeks and then each ward sister made out a report on our progress, just like school.

My second ward was full of teenagers suffering from polio. Some were in iron lungs while others wore callipers and were learning to walk again. The RNO had a large physiotherapy department and swimming pool. This dreadful disease generally afflicted the most athletic teenagers. A few years later in 1955 an American doctor called Jonas Salk produced a polio vaccine. Although he was hailed as a miracle worker he had no wish to make monetary benefit from his discovery: he simply wanted to eradicate the disease world wide. Generally I think his wish has been achieved. Our son Malcolm's generation was among the first to benefit.

We worked a five and half day week from 8am to 8 pm with three hours off each day, plus tea breaks and half an hour lunch break. We learnt to be quick and thorough at all times. Three minutes for two nurses to make a bed! I loved every minute of my working day. My friends gave me two nick names, 'Mo', because of my Irish surname, Maloney, and 'Legs' because of those pretty cami-knickers which I wore when off duty.

Almost all nursing staff were female, residential and unmarried. In eighteen months I met only one male nurse. The only young men of my age that I met who were not patients were a troop of Sea Scouts who used to visit the hospital periodically as volunteers. In those early days of the NHS ward sisters were responsible for all staff working on their ward, and patients were allowed to smoke, but few did. Nurses were never allowed to sit on a patient's bed. The only time student nurses were allowed to sit down or to smoke cigarettes was when we were in the ward office on night duty and it was then that Dossie and I began to smoke Du Maurier cigarettes to keep awake in the early hours of the morning. Visiting hours were limited to three times a week and only two visitors were allowed at one time. Two stools were provided for them to sit on. Children under thirteen were not allowed to visit at any time. Looking back now, it seems very harsh but at the time it was accepted.

Outside the hospital a bus stop connected with the underground railway at Edgware. Nearby were Cannons Park and the church of St Lawrence where my mother lay buried. Occasionally I attended a service there. The high wrought iron gates of the hospital were locked at 11 30pm every night and Dad warned me that if we missed the last bus after a night out in London we must not accept a lift from a motorist. It was, and still is, a lonely place. When we missed the last bus and could not afford a taxi between us, we walked up Brockley Hill. Then the only way to get into the hospital without detection was to climb over the wall into the nurses' home. I only did it once as I am not good at heights and as I did so Night Sister grabbed my leg. Next morning I was summoned to Matron's office to be reprimanded.

Dad helped me to buy a new Raleigh cycle on hire purchase, enabling me to tour the grounds and local countryside with my friend Ruth. Once she fell off her cycle on Brockley Hill and I had to call an ambulance to pick her up. Sometimes I cycled home to Edgware. The RNO had a tennis court and Winnie gave me her tennis racquet, but I never enjoyed playing. Years later I found it much more fun to see professionals play at Wimbledon or watch it on television. Once, after a weekend away, Dizzie returned wearing a pair of slacks, as women's trousers were called in those days. Next morning she was summoned to the Matron's office and told that nurses were not allowed to wear trousers within the hospital grounds. It seems strange in this twenty first century because women of all ages now wear trousers most of the time, but in 1949 it was most uncommon. Dad would certainly not allow me or Anne to wear them. He always said 'I wear the trousers in this house!' and it was six years before Anne or I wore them.

Generally we students spent our days off in London town in uniform, frequently lunching at Lyons Corner House in the Strand after calling at a ticket agency in Trafalgar Square, which provided students with free tickets for the best seats at all of London's theatres and the opportunity to see all the famous plays and musicals of the day like Oklahoma, Carousel and South Pacific. The London Palladium and The Windmill Theatre were very popular, because the American singers and comedians performed there; at The Windmill Theatre then, statuesque immobile nude show girls stood at the back of the stage during performances. Once, I took my brother Terry there with me and we sat in the front stalls listening to the American singer Billy Daniels give his popular rendition of That Old Black Magic.

One afternoon in mufti I stood near a news vendor in Piccadilly Circus waiting for friends to meet me, when a pretty young woman wearing heavy makeup approached me and said in a threatening voice 'If you do not move off my patch, I will get someone to use a razor on your face.' I was stunned and moved very quickly. She obviously thought I was a Lady of the Town!

Sometimes I stayed overnight with, or brought home with me one of my nursing friends to stay the night. My bedroom now had twin beds and occasionally Dad took in a female lodger to help pay the bills. I went to Wimbledon tennis club with Joy and Dossie and once I spent the day at the Oval cricket ground sitting on hassocks on the grass near the gasometers in front of the boundary ropes, watching Len Hutton play for England in a Test Match. Dad was green with envy, because he had to work. He loved cricket and often came home at lunch time to listen to John Arlott the cricket commentator on the wireless. There were no transistor radios then.

NIGHT DUTY

By the autumn of 1949 I had worked on two wards and attended several surgical operations. Dossie knew I hated large moths almost as much as bats and out of sheer devilment, while I was downstairs in the lobby on the public telephone to my father, she entered my room in the nurses' home and left my light on with the window wide open; I returned to discover a room full of large moths.

The next day our group went on night duty, working a twelve hour shift from 8pm. On night duty we students dealt with bedpans, pressure areas and hot drinks and in cold weather we also filled stone hot water bottles for patients in spinal beds. Generally there were one or two students and a staff nurse to each ward. My first ward was female where most of my patients lay in spinal plaster casts or hip spicas. All the adult wards had been Nissen huts built for use by the armed forces during the second world war: each one had a coal stove in the centre which gave off a certain amount of heat but in cold weather they were not ideal either for patients or staff. On my first night before we started our shift my staff nurse took me to the ward kitchen and searched for and found a cracked cup and said 'If things get hectic I will come and smash that cup!' and ever since, I have disliked cracked cups, too.

At Halloween Dossie and I went round the Nurses' Home together and made apple pie beds in every room including Night Sister's. Dossie went on to work at the Bristol Royal Infirmary and in 1953 she married a doctor working there. I was ill in hospital at the time and could not attend their wedding. I had several operations and they sent me fruit and flowers from Harrods. I could not afford to shop in Harrods and I was very impressed. Shortly afterwards she wrote to tell me that her husband's brother had committed suicide. Sadly, because of my ill health we completely lost touch. I could not remember her new surname and I sometimes wonder if she might live in Bristol and that perhaps she has grandchildren that play with my grandchildren.

One night I was put in charge of my ward and had to call my staff nurse to attend an elderly patient being treated for a fractured femur; she was vomiting and complaining of violent stomach ache. The house doctor was summoned and at midnight I accompanied the poor lady to the operating theatre where she had a colostomy. I spent the rest of the night at her bed side. She was aged 56 and looked very old. She died two days later and I was very sad.

On my first night on a male ward I was very apprehensive when with a pounding heart I carried round a crate of urinals. However, the male patients, many of whom were old enough to be my father, were kind and I liked working there. Before bedding them down for the night we had to go round and treat pressure areas. A very handsome young man in his early twenties asked me to rub his left heel. I pulled back his covers and found he did not have a left leg. He laughed when he saw my shocked face. He explained he still felt his foot even though it had been amputated.

Children's wards were my favourite on night duty, especially where there were babies. Once I shared an office with the male staff nurse working on the adjoining ward and one night when he had gone for a dinner break I checked his patients, all young boys suffering from spinal problems, many of whom were strapped to iron frames. I found one of them crying in great distress and from what he told me the male nurse had been behaving improperly. I reported it to Night Sister and his behaviour was observed and he was quickly dismissed.

Our nursing group was given three weeks' annual leave over Christmas 1949 and New Year 1950. I went home. Typical of many in the building trade, Dad decided to work at home on Christmas Eve and installed a new fireplace with an all night coal fire in our dining room. Thank goodness it was completed that day and the warmth permeated through the whole house and gave us constant hot water over the festive season.

NEW DECADE

After Christmas my nursing friend Rowena invited me to spend two weeks at her home in the village of Abridge in Essex and on New Year's Eve a party was held at her home which ended at midnight. There I was introduced to a drink called the Green Goddess which made me tipsy and I made the mistake of bragging that I could waltz on ice skates, which was not true! The following morning, New Year's Day 1950, Rowena and her friends decided we would all go ice skating at Wembley Ice Rink. When we got there I put on hired skates, while Rowena and her friends had brought their own, for they were expert skaters and most had learnt to ski in the Swiss Alps. Almost immediately they discovered that I had been misleading them about my talent for skating. Gran Hill would have said 'Be sure your sins will find you out.' As a punishment I was taken to the middle of the ice rink by two handsome lads and left there. It taught me a lesson. Fortunately I was forgiven and on 13th January Rowena and I went with her parents to a Hunt Ball in Chigwell. I had borrowed a blue ball gown for the occasion from one of our neighbours in Edgware and I adored dancing all night with Rowena's family friends and we walked through the village to her home at 3 am. I had never been out so late in my life.

During the spring of 1950 Dad and Arthur set up in business together, Arthur as carpenter and Dad as painter and decorator. To help get to and from work with tools they bought a second hand Daimler shooting brake with leather seats and dashboard, which Dad kept it in our garage at Raeburn Road. Terry told me recently that shortly after it arrived Dad suggested they go out for a drive together and as they drove through Edgware Terry remarked 'This is the way I go to visit Mummy's grave.' Dad said nothing until they arrived at the church. Then he slowed down, pulled up at the curb outside the lych-gate and said, 'Come on, come with me!' With his arm wrapped around Terry he took him unerringly straight to Mummy's grave. They stood there and his arm got so tight around Terry that he told me he thought he would break in half. He looked at Dad and saw tears running down his face and after a few minutes he said 'Let's go. Please don't tell Auntie, will you?' They never

Me ready for dancing!

spoke of it again and I knew nothing about it.

A hospital ball was held at the RNO and Dad was so proud of Anne's achievement in making me an off the shoulder long white lace gown for the event, with a little cape and long white mittens, that he asked our neighbour Mr Smith, an amateur photographer, to take a photograph of me wearing it. I never liked it: I much preferred the fabulous white gown Dizzie wore which probably cost a great deal of money. The orthopaedic consultant Professor Cholmondley invited me to dance that evening and we won a prize of a china vase, which I cherished for many years. Now it is long gone. Afterwards, while we were walking back to the nurses' home through the hospital grounds in the moonlight that night, May bugs attached themselves to our gowns; they reminded me of bats and I became hysterical!

CHAPTER EIGHTEEN

Problems

In the summer I began to complain of abdominal pain and sought the medical advice of the hospital doctor. He examined me twice, and asked me if I had been behaving improperly with any young man, implying that I was pregnant. I laughed at the absurdity of his remark, because I was so naive and did not have any boy friends. In those days there was no test for pregnancy. When I told Dad he sent me to our family doctor, who immediately made the correct diagnosis: I had an ovarian cyst the size of a large grapefruit removed at Edgware General hospital and after I had sat my exams I was advised against continuing with orthopaedic nursing as my general health was low.

I was sent to convalesce at a small holding in Four Marks, Hampshire. The weather was sunny and dry and for two weeks I and all the other residents ate most of our meals, except breakfast, in the garden under the apple trees. The fresh air gave us enormous appetites and during the day I helped feed pigs, ducks, chickens and goats and every night before sleeping in camp beds we had biscuits and a glass of milk. While I was staying there I visited Jane Austen's house and Winchester cathedral. Dad and Anne came to fetch me home in the Daimler and we toured the beautiful city of Winchester before driving home.

Whenever we attended the chest clinic at Edgware hospital for our six monthly check up, it was so crowded with patients waiting for x-rays we spent most of the day there. In the late summer Lizzie and Jim, who were visiting auntie Mary and family at Tunbridge Wells, came over to see us in Edgware. Lizzie looked tiny as she stood beside Terry who was almost sixteen years old and nearly six foot tall. Dad took our photo in the garden with them and I realise now that Terry looked gaunt and ill.

HANWELL

I was absolutely delighted to get a letter from Addie to say that she and Tom and little Bobby were now living at Hanwell in west London which was accessible by bus.

Many years later Tom told me the saga of how he obtained this home for his little family. After he came out of the Fleet Air Arm in early 1947, he tried to find a job and a home in London for himself and his family. Accommodation was hard to find since so much of London lay in ruins because of bomb damage. Friends of his, who lived in west London, found him a grotty basement room in Westbourne Grove so that he could claim residency and establish a base from which to make application for a council house in the area for himself, his wife and his son. He found a job but had little money to visit Addie and Bobby in Wales, and they endured three years of separation.

A Labour government was in power and in desperation Tom wrote to several Labour MPs for their help, including the Housing Minister in Atlee's Labour Government, thinking quite naturally that they were there to help ex-service men. He received a sympathetic reply from the Housing Minister, but one MP replied saying 'We have a long waiting list of people and we have so many who are homeless and seeking accommodation.' He said the government had many West Indians who needed housing too. This was hard for Tom to swallow. He replied that he had given six years of his life for his country and got little thanks for it. However, eventually he was housed on the Cuckoo Hill estate in the London borough of Ealing in 1950 but always resented the way he had been forced to wait.

I was impatient to see them, so at the first opportunity I took a chance one weekend hoping that they would all be at home, and caught a bus to Ealing and then a single decker to the Cuckoo Hill Estate, at Hanwell. There I found them at 48 Stephenson Road. Most of the houses were identical and I was pleased to see their home was a corner terrace house with a front door at the side overlooking a little green, which gave it some individuality and privacy.

At the other end of their road, beyond some open fields, stood an old building which was all that remained of the Central London District School known as Cuckoo Schools. It was opened in 1856 to take children from the workhouses of central London and Southwark. The 1,000 children who settled there then, together with members of staff, doubled the population of Hanwell overnight. Cuckoo Schools was pulled down in 1933 to make way for the council to build the Cuckoo Estate. The most famous of the Cuckoo Schools' children was Charlie Chaplin, and the reception block of Cuckoo Schools still remains as a Community Centre. In 2002 Cousin Bobby told me it had been used recently as background in a film.

Addie and Tom's home consisted of two bedrooms with a loo upstairs, while downstairs there were a small entrance hall, a living room, a kitchen and a small bathroom. Their kitchen was very basic with a sink unit under the window that looked out on to a small back garden. They had no fridge or washing machine - few people did then. Tom was not fond of gardening but Addie always enjoyed it. She had several cuttings of flowering plants taken from Rhandir Delyn and she grew runner beans.

Their living room, with comfortable furniture, like most homes in the fifties had a coal fire but no central heating. Above the open fire place was a large round mirror with which I was familiar most of my life, though it was only in 2002 that Bobby told me it was a wedding present to Addie and Tom from my parents.

They invited me to stay with them for a few days and whenever I did so Tom gave up his bed and slept in their living room on a bed settee, so that I could sleep in comfort with Addie. I felt very much at home, immediately recognising the dressing table, tallboy and wardrobe in their bedroom which had been in Rhandir Delyn during my childhood. Tom went to work at 6 30am every weekday, and before doing so he lit the oil stove in the kitchen on cold days and always brought Addie a cup of tea in bed! Whenever I slept there I got one too. On one such visit I was wearing Addie's satin night gown which she had worn on her honeymoon, and as I sat up in bed and sleepily took the cup of tea that Tom offered me I accidentally threw it over my shoulder and the shock catapulted Addie and me from the bed! We all laughed a lot about it, later!

Staying with them was a pleasure. It was a happy home and I loved being there. Little Bobby, at five years of age, was a dear little redhead with boundless energy. When he was still, he liked me to read Noddy books to him and I took him to school walking through an avenue of horse chestnut trees and collected conkers on the way back because Addie said they kept her clothes free of moths. Then we quickly did the housework and took a bus to Ealing, which was a thriving shopping centre with large department stores. Tom returned from work around 5 pm each day and Addie always cooked an evening meal. Afterwards they washed the dishes together while listening to a popular radio programme called 'The Archers' which ran for fifteen minutes every week day evening and still does in the twenty first century.

BLACK AND WHITE TELEVISION

Back in 1926 a Scot by the name of John Logie Baird was the first to publicly demonstrate television in his small laboratory in the Soho district of London and in the next ten years or so moving pictures were being transmitted to a very limited area of London. But the second world war put a stop to the progress that was being made in this new medium. After the war, in 1949, black and white television sets began to be mass produced and were obtainable in electrical shops. Winnie and Arthur were among the first to buy one and they invited us and their neighbours in to their sitting room to see this new phenomenon on a nine-inch screen, which was very exciting. At first, programmes, which consisted mainly of news, were short and took place in the early evening. Television had to be viewed in a darkened room or in the dark. An interval was provided, long enough to switch on the electric light and make and drink a cup of tea.

Before television sets appeared in the average home sitting rooms were not used except on Sundays and festive occasions but this new medium was best viewed from a comfortable armchair and it quickly became popular throughout the land, slowly transforming most people's life style.

Many families who normally went to the cinema at least twice a week bought a television and gradually as the length and diversity of programmes increased transmission improved sufficiently to allow a small lamp to remain lit while viewing and people began to stay home and make their sitting rooms comfortable places in which to relax and went less often to the theatre, cinema and dances. In 1951 Dad bought a television and our three piece suite in the sitting room came into everyday use for the first time. It began to be a must-have product in every home. Now fifty years later television is a universal institution and most families in this country have at least one in their homes.

CHANGING FASHION

Before the days of package holidays abroad, female fashion in Britain in the early fifties was feminine and colourful, with skirts just below the knee. High heels were popular and as tights had not yet been invented, women wore nylon stockings with seams, held up by suspender belts, and seldom, if ever, went barelegged, unless poverty stricken, or at the seaside in summertime. Little white gloves were highly fashionable and I always carried a spare pair in my handbag. I still liked hats but seldom wore one. Trilby hats were less common for men than they had been in the thirties and many men and women went bareheaded. Men usually wore suits and ties, or blazers with grey slacks, and younger men began to wear belts rather than braces and most males walked courteously on the outside of the pavement when escorting females and when it rained they still wore the perennial trench coat.

People were generally neat and tidy, well behaved and polite with strangers and queued quietly when necessary. Black faces were comparatively rare and foreigners were uncommon. Children were mostly seen and not heard in public. It was generations before graffiti and beggars appeared on the streets of London and other cities.

Supermarkets were unheard of and the first time I saw a small shop with such a facility in Watling Avenue in Burnt Oak everyone said it would become a great temptation for thieves. Only ice-cream cones were eaten in the street. Far more men than women smoked cigarettes and women seldom did so in the street so litter was very light and consisted mainly of 'fag ends'. Public houses closed at 10.30pm and women seldom entered one without a male escort. It was not the done thing. Most streets were deserted by 11pm. Public transport was good and everyone queued quietly and politely to board buses, all of which had conductors on board to collect fares.

Buses and tube trains were particularly busy at the beginning and end of the working day and also when the cinemas and public houses closed for the night. The police were well respected and because they could be plainly seen walking in the streets of London, Dad often told me that if I got lost I should 'Ask a policeman!'

I had a number of boy friends; and that summer aged nineteen I began to suffer from insomnia. For a short time I thought I was in love and Dad came to my room late one night, sat on my bed talking to me in the dark and said he was concerned about me for he did not want me to have a serious relationship with a boy as I was too young and he suggested I do nothing in haste! I assured him he need not worry, I was just out to enjoy myself, and going to concerts. He seemed relieved and said 'I think twenty five is a good age to marry and settle down.' I realised auntie Anne was about that age when she met Dad. It never occurred to me to point out to him that when my mother married him she was only twenty years old.

One of my boyfriends liked classical music and took me to Promenade Concerts at the Albert Hall where I developed a particular liking for Beethoven and adored the Hebridean Overture by Mendelssohn. I had seen a film about the Scottish islands including Staffa at the Adelphi Cinema in Edgware and as soon as I heard this beautiful music I vowed that one day I would go there to see the island for myself.

COUSIN BETTY

In October that year I had a week's annual leave and I went down to Margate again to stay with Mary and Jim. They had no holiday makers staying as the summer season was over. My cousin Betty, Bessie's daughter, came up from Wales to spend a few days with me. She was now a pretty fifteen year old blonde with a great sense of humour and a ready laugh. Most places open to tourists were closed, but never mind, we enjoyed ourselves. We had the run of the town and the promenade. I felt very worldly compared with my young cousin and some days we fought a blustery wind as we amused ourselves in the cafés and arcades along Margate sea front.

We both had good appetites and Jim was an excellent chef, so we were well fed. In the evenings, with our little cousins in bed, we were able to enjoy the company of Mary and Jim, and when we retired to the large double bed we shared, Betty and I would lie awake for hours talking. I told her what little I knew of the facts of life. We never had much sleep because we became quite hysterical with laughter. At the end of our holiday Betty returned with me on the train to London and at Victoria station Dad met us both in the Daimler shooting brake and drove us ten miles home to Edgware to be greeted by Anne and Terry. While Anne was in the kitchen making a cup of tea for us Dad stood silently looking at Betty under the lamp light in our dining room. I thought he looked very odd: he was grey in the face which was most unusual, for he had a ruddy complexion. It occurred to me he might be ill: perhaps my nursing experience had made me more observant. But when he spoke I realised what was wrong. 'Betty,' he said, in a strangled voice, 'has anyone ever told you that you look like your auntie Ann?' I realised immediately he was talking about my mother and that he was emotionally upset. I glanced at Betty, seeing her with fresh eyes: at fifteen she was lovely with a heart shaped face and except for the colour of her eyes and blonde hair I could see a striking family resemblance. After all, she was Mummy's niece. I do not recollect Betty's reply. Next day Dad took her to Paddington station and put her on the train to Wales.

At the age of nineteen, after approximately two years in Orthopaedic nursing, I was advised by Dr. Trenchard my tuberculosis consultant to take some leave: for a few weeks I remained at home just helping Anne with the housework while we listened to Housewives Choice on the wireless. I showed her how to make the beds with hospital corners. Then after a coffee break she spent the rest of the day dressmaking for customers and she made me a fashionable grey pinafore dress and jacket. Dad wanted us all to emigrate and we went to Rhodesia House in London: however nothing came of his dream because Terry and I did not pass the medical examination.

CHAPTER NINETEEN

Return to Nursing

Anxious to return to nursing I discussed my career prospects with Dr Trenchard and because of my persistence, at his recommendation I became a student nurse caring for patients with pulmonary tuberculosis at Colindale Hospital. Transport from home was easy, one stop from Burnt Oak tube station. I was fitted out with blue and white striped uniform dresses and small stiff white caps, minus aprons. I provided my own black shoes and stockings.

On reflection, I now think I was somewhat foolhardy. I had already spent six months in a sanatorium after appearing to be infected with the disease and it was only five years since it had killed my mother: although I did not know it, just months after she died the life of a twenty one year-old American woman had been miraculously saved by a new drug called Streptomycin. Like my mother, she had been suffering from the advanced stages of the disease. Consequently this drug was now being used regularly in the treatment of tuberculosis, but even so it would be two years or more before additional miracle drugs in combination with surgery would eradicate TB permanently from Great Britain, or so everyone thought .

Colindale Hospital was roughly two miles from my home, situated beside the tube station of that name, opposite the Newspaper Library and Public Health Laboratory and near Hendon police training college and Hendon aerodrome. Its 280 beds were devoted almost entirely to the treatment of pulmonary tuberculosis and the vast majority of patients were male, with the exception of two ten bedded female wards.

Most were ex-Prisoners of War or former servicemen of World War Two: at first allowed up only to wash and use the loo, the majority took at least six months to recover on bed rest with daily medication and injections of streptomycin plus minor surgery, with a rest hour in the middle of the day, when there was silence while they lay reading or listening to the radio on ear phones. Visiting hours: two visitors per patient from 2 to 4pm Tuesday and Thursday and one hour on Saturday and Sunday evenings; children under the age of thirteen were forbidden to visit; and one ward was used for patients requiring major surgery.

Fresh air was considered very important in the treatment of tuberculosis and windows remained open except in bad weather. All wards had three centrally heated side rooms for the very ill but main wards had only a coal stove. Each ward had three open air balconies each containing the beds of two patients. The exceptions to this rule were the single orthopaedic ward which had one balcony and the women's wards which had no balconies. During winter months the balcony patients slept under sheepskins with tarpaulin covers and wind breaks. There was a day room, where ambulant patients, up for one or two hours, could sit, relax and play games like shove hapenny, monopoly, cribbage or whist.

As patients recuperated they were allowed to get up and dress for lengthening periods of time and were encouraged to do occupational therapy, such as making lamp shades, weaving scarves and making tapestries on frame; and when they were allowed to dress for several hours they could attend patients' whist drives once a week. Also, weather permitting, they were allowed to walk about the hospital and grounds. A few weeks prior to discharge, if their chest X-rays, blood tests and sputum were clear they were allowed out into the community again: at first for just a one hour pass; then over the next few weeks the time was increased until they were allowed to visit their homes a couple of times for a whole week-end, after which they were discharged fit. Many patients said the first time they left the hospital after months of confinement they felt a bit like lepers and as they walked up Colindale Avenue, they wanted to shout 'Unclean! Unclean!'

SURGICAL WARD

I started work part time on the thirty bed surgical ward, gradually building up to full time. The sister was a charming, plump Irish woman, and the most popular staff nurse was an Irishman. My first duty was to blanket bath an elderly man recovering from surgery. On all wards when treating patients at close quarters, all staff wore cotton masks and a white cotton gown on top of uniforms. Plastic aprons and gloves did not exist in the nineteen fifties.

Each patient had his own Fahrenheit glass thermometer kept in disinfectant in a test tube above his bed. It was placed under his tongue for three minutes night and morning while his pulse and respiration were counted and charted for one minute. it took some time to complete and fill in all the patients' charts. While we were doing so, it was a great opportunity for the nurse to help patients with crossword puzzles in the daily newspapers.

Near the sister's office at the entrance to all the male wards and

Colindale Hospital.

opposite the staff loo and a blanket cupboard was the nurses' work-room, containing a sink, soap and nail brush so that nurses could scrub their hands for several minutes in running water. Taps could be turned on and off with elbows so that hands were as clean as possible before doing patients' dressings. The room held a sterilis-er with boiling water and a large pair of forceps to remove instru-ments from it; a glass cabinet with shelves in which to store them; a dressings trolley, syringes, steel drums containing dressings and swabs, replenished when necessary and sent to the autoclave by night staff; and most important of all, a medicine cupboard - no medicine trolleys or pre-packed dressings in those days.

Nurses donned a mask and scrubbed their hands for several minutes with the nail brush before and after handling sterile dressing with forceps and treating patients. Every ward had ample facilities for this and it was extremely important to keep finger nails short. The patients' toilet was at the far end of each ward beside a sluice room where bedpans were washed, urine tests were made and dirty linen and sputum pots were stored until porters collected them.

Chest surgery was generally performed under a local anaesthetic even when removing a whole lung, so a nurse familiar to the patient accompanied him to theatre, and sat beside him holding his hand and comforting him throughout the operation in a temperature above ninety degrees and all staff wore light weight clothing under their gowns, with caps and masks, while white boots replaced their shoes. Only surgeons and the nurses actually assisting them wore gloves. Some lungs when removed were a very dark grey instead of pink in colour, usually indicating the patient was a heavy smoker. Post operatively patients were nursed in side rooms and for the first two weeks had intensive physiotherapy including the tipping of beds on blocks to help free lungs of congestion, when sputum pots were copiously filled.

One day as I began my walk down the long hospital corridor to the changing room in the nurses' home, I passed a handsome young Irish priest who ministered to the Catholics among the patients and staff. As my father was a Catholic I said 'Hello, Father.' He pursued me the length of the corridor, until I explained that during the Second World War I had lived with relatives in Wales and had been confirmed in the Church in Wales.

On the early shift, starting at 8am after serving breakfast, making beds, taking patients' observations, medicines and injections, I helped collect up and replace tin sputum pots from every locker which went to be sterilised. Then a complete silence always descended upon the ward. During the late morning rest hour nursing staff moved about quietly. One day I scolded a young man walking out of the day room instead of lying on his bed, telling him he should know better, then I noticed he had a stethoscope round his neck! The following morning this young doctor collared me to take a patient's blood under his supervision which I managed with some trepidation for I had never done so before.

Once a week student nurses, most of whom were female, attended lectures given by a sister tutor and a doctor. I found my knowledge of anatomy and physiology learnt at the Royal National Orthopaedic hospital very helpful. On average the students of both sexes at Colindale were in their late twenties and less well educated than the RNO students, though some were already qualified state registered nurses.

In the early years of the National Health Service a Matron was the chief administrator in each hospital and an extremely powerful individual. They sometimes breathed holy terror into their nursing staff. Ward sisters were entirely responsible for the running of their particular ward and all staff working there, including the cleaners. Sisters sometimes got wind of Matron's imminent arrival and being forewarned all staff were prepared. Our matron, a Miss Ward, was an Irishwoman.

I thoroughly enjoyed being back in nursing. Life was good, I was happy and extremely energetic and occasionally cycled to the hospital from home. The patients appreciated all that was done for them: I remember once, try as I might using all my feminine guile,

Me on left with two friends outside main entrance of Colindale hospital.

I just could not persuade a patient to eat his rice pudding. He refused point blank. Later the ward Sister explained that he had been a prisoner of the Japanese working on the Thai - Burma railway. I went to the public library to do research about it and was distressed when I read the stark description of the atrocities inflicted on Prisoners of War and just how many of them died while building that railway. No wonder he couldn't face eating rice. I remember his name to this day: it was Richard Stockford.

241

After three months I was transferred to a medical ward; on my first shift the sister, about to go off duty, told me I would find the nurse in charge in the blanket cupboard. There I found her bending over near the floor but when she raised her pretty head minus a cap I realised she was a he - a very feminine looking male staff nurse, with fabulously long eyelashes. I made friends among the nursing staff and Vera Jenkins, a Welsh girl, became my special friend. At weekends we began to go dancing together with her boy friend Bert, whom she married later that year.

Meanwhile Anne decided to give up working from home to become manageress of a haberdashery and material shop in Burnt Oak Broadway. I called to see her there one day and she introduced me to a young man who worked for her, called Alan. Vera and Bert called to see her at the shop and met Alan who told Bert he liked ballroom dancing. Bert invited him to come dancing with us and for a few weeks every Saturday night we met Alan at the Welsh Harp ballroom in Colindale. Apart from nursing and cycling, dancing was the love of my life, particularly when dancing the Gay Gordons. It did not take long for me to realise Alan had hoped Anne would come dancing too. He was totally enamoured of her and talked about her all the time and sometimes called me Anne. He lived in Battersea and always walked me home afterwards, in hopes he would be invited in. I don't think Anne or Dad ever knew how he felt.

CHRISTMAS 1951

In the winter of 1951, as the festive season approached, we decorated our ward with garlands to help lift the spirits of staff and patients and we made a mock mantelpiece above the coal stove in the ward with stockings for Santa Claus hanging from it. As another student nurse and I said good night before going off duty at the end of the day shift on Christmas Eve there was a sudden commotion and we paused. Some of the patients were pointing to a piece of mistletoe hanging up in front of the fireplace. 'Please will one of you kiss one of us under the mistletoe?' they chorused. My colleague, also aged nineteen, had a pronounced stammer and was new to the ward. We stood there hesitantly, and I realised it would make them happy if I had the courage to do as they requested. A patient who had been told he could go home for a few hours on Christmas Day itself and would be discharged in the New Year came forward in his dressing gown. I felt obliged to volunteer and loud cheering broke out as we kissed very briefly. After supper in the staff dining room I joined a group of nurses carrying lanterns and wearing our navy and red cloaks we sang Christmas carols at all ward doorways and my thoughts were of auntie Lizzie and midnight mass at St Mary's in Burry Port.

In the early nineteen fifties Christmas for most people in Great Britain was just a two day Bank holiday, then back to work unless a Sunday followed on. Nursing staff at Colindale worked from 8am to 8pm on one of the festive days. I chose to work on Christmas Day itself: leaving Terry, Dad and Anne still snug in bed I walked down to Burnt Oak tube station in the early morning, meeting the postman on his rounds and the milkman with his horse and cart, for they both worked on Christmas Day in those days. The ward atmosphere was festive as we served breakfast and during our coffee break a colleague invited me and the pretty male staff nurse with whom I worked to go to her room in the Nurses Home to see her Christmas presents. He was totally captivated by the fabulous lingerie she had received and held some of her frilly French knickers against himself, bemoaning the fact that he could not wear them. I thought it was very sad, for he was such a nice person: he told us his parents longed for the day when he would get married, but he had no wish to do so. Homosexuality was illegal in the early fifties and at the time I knew little about it. I often wonder what happened to him.

A long trestle table was erected down the centre of every ward on Christmas day and most of our patients were able to sit out to eat their Christmas dinner; Dr. Trenchard came to carve an enormous turkey and it was a happy occasion, with photographs taken by one of the patients.

Dad and Anne were holding a party on the evening of Boxing Day and as it was my day off Terry and I helped them prepare for it. Dad rolled back the carpet in the dining room ready for dancing and put a barrel of beer with some spirits and glasses in our hall. In the late afternoon as he drove me to a boy friend's home for the evening he complained of a headache, which was most unusual

The weather was murky and our Daimler shooting brake crawled along in a fog so thick that Dad hit the curb once or twice and for the last half mile I got out to guide him with the aid of a large torch. When we reached our destination, he stumbled as he walked me to the door of the house and I began to wonder if there was something wrong with him. There were no drink and drive laws in those days but I knew that he hadn't drunk any alcohol that day. I was worried about him and my boy friend's parents let me phone home to check he had returned safely.

Later, when I returned home by taxi, I was amazed to discover even though Anne was up and guests were still in the house, like

Terry, my Dad was already in bed. One of his cronies paid my taxi driver, and shortly afterwards all the guests departed and Anne and I retired for the night. The following morning Dad went to see our doctor who diagnosed concussion after a fall down stairs on Christmas morning, of which I knew nothing and he spent the rest of that day lying down in a darkened room.

NEW YEAR 1952

In the early New Year of 1952 I was transferred to another medical ward and during my lunch break a colleague told me there were some photos of the Christmas festivities on sale in my previous ward, and I went along to see them. The patient who had taken them had a dozen or so small black and white prints mounted on a board; there was one of Dr. Trenchard carving the turkey at the head of the trestle table and centrally placed I spotted a photo of a patient kissing a nurse who was practically hidden from view. Though the nurse was unrecognisable I realised it was me, taken on Christmas Eve; I had not realised a photo had been taken. I ordered some photographs and returned to my ward where the Sister informed me that Matron wished to see me at once. When I was seated in front of her with both hands together in my lap, as nurses were expected to behave in her presence, she said 'My assistant matron has seen a photo of a nurse kissing a patient on Ward Six, and on enquiring who the nurse was she was told it was you. Was it you?'

'Yes. it was,' I replied.

'Why did you do it?' she asked in an accusing voice.

Feeling somewhat flustered I said 'I did it in the heat of the moment!'

She then asked 'In the heat of what moment, Nurse?'

So I told her 'It was Christmas Eve, the patients asked for a volunteer, I did it to cheer them up!'

I was shocked to hear her say that the patient involved was at that very moment being interviewed by the hospital's senior consultant and faced the possibility of immediate discharge. 'If so, Nurse, you will be dismissed!'

Mortified, I left her office in tears and went straight home to tell Dad what had happened, and he told me to contact the Nurses' Union, but I didn't need to, for on further enquiry my behaviour was recognised as an innocent if foolish gesture, and nothing more was said and the patient left the hospital in good health a couple of weeks later.

Meantime Matron transferred me to a medical ward run by Sister Bowyer, a cantankerous old biddie, a strong disciplinarian with a fierce reputation: she had obviously been instructed to keep an eye on me! She was known throughout the hospital as 'The Old Grey Mare'. Small of stature and nearing retirement, she took an instant dislike to me and after only a few days I began to feel persecuted. It seemed that in her eyes I could do nothing right. If anything went wrong in ward routine when I was on duty, she held me responsible, frequently chastising me in front of staff, and sometimes even in the middle of the ward in front of the patients.

I endured several weeks of this treatment in silence, finally cracking one morning. I turned on my heel and went straight to her office leaving her bellowing in the ward. She followed me indignantly, on her little legs, and when the door shut behind us, I told her 'If you wish to reprimand me, this is where you should do it.'

Me on ward six.

Next day one of my colleagues told me that Sister Bowyer was a devout Protestant, with a strong prejudice against Catholics. This fact was made abundantly clear when she called me into her office to tell me that she had given me the following Saturday night off - St Patrick's Day - '....so that you can go to Confession, Nurse'.

I completely lost my temper and said 'How dare you suggest I need to go to Confession? As it happens my father is a Catholic, but I am a confirmed member of the Church of England despite having an Irish surname: but either way, it is the same God we worship.'

Her jaw fell open and she said 'Oh! you have a voice!'

From that day on I could do no wrong in her eyes. Despite her quarrelsome nature she was a good nursing sister. Taking me under her wing she taught me a lot. After that incident if any member of her ward staff wanted a favour, they would ask me to intercede on their behalf. During Coronation year she received a medal in recognition of long service and she gave me a Nurses' Prayer Book.

I was feeling much happier and just before Easter 1952 Dad raised no objections when I took up residence at the nurses' home. Sister Bowyer gave me most of that Easter weekend off, so I spent it in Thanet staying with Mary, Jim and children. On Easter Saturday my cousin John Thomas picked me up and took me to watch him and his friends play hockey at Manston airport, and that evening I went dancing with them at Dreamland Ballroom in Margate, and afterwards one of John's friends walked me back to Mary's house.

In the fifties every one 'got the key of the door' on reaching their majority at the age of twenty one. Now the age has been lowered to eighteen. My friend Joy, by this time doing her State Registration at University College Hospital in Euston, celebrated her twenty first birthday that May: I attended a tea party at her home in Bushey after which we all went to see a play at the Palace Theatre in Watford and the next time I saw Dad I persuaded him to give me a small party at the Piccadilly hotel in London for my twenty first birthday the following year.

I had a good social life and when the telephone rang at home in the evening or at weekends it was usually for me, with a choice of invitations. I attended a Wimbledon tennis tournament, visited London theatres, concert halls, cinemas, restaurants and ballrooms with my nursing colleagues past and present or boy friends, but I had not lost my heart yet. There was no one extra special and nothing very serious.

For one month I worked in the operating theatre learning how to help keep things running smoothly, like counting swabs and placing them on hooks after use in operations and holding dishes for the surgeons when they removed ribs or parts of lungs. Once, in the middle of such an operation the surgeon, Mr Jackson, asked me 'How would you like this operation, Nurse?'

I was horrified, and told him 'It would be a nightmare.'

CHAPTER TWENTY

A New Patient

During the summer months, coming and going on my way in and out of the hospital, and quite a distance from all the wards I frequently saw a bronzed fair haired orthopaedic patient in a hip spica plaster cast, stripped to the waist lying on his bed in the sunshine. He was seldom alone when I passed by; almost Invariably he had either his mother sitting beside him or two or more doting nurses standing round, who would later rave about him at meal times in the staff canteen. I discovered his name was David Sinclair. One day he was no longer there and I heard that he had had an operation on his hip.

A few weeks later on my day off as I made my way out of the hospital via the staff garden separated by a privet hedge from the small balcony of the orthopaedic ward, I noticed David Sinclair sitting there reading a newspaper and as I passed he lowered his paper and stared at me until I disappeared from view. This act made me feel uncomfortable. The expression on his face gave me the impression that he thought I was something the cat had brought in. I decided that even though he was handsome I did not like him in the very least!

During their training state registered student nurses from Edgware General came to work at Colindale Hospital for three months and one of them, a redhead called Sheila, worked on that orthopaedic ward for most of the time. She was a stylish girl with long

David with his mother in the grounds of Colindale hospital.

red hair and an unusual dress sense. She took a shine to a patient called Olie and he took a shine to her, too. They 'went over the wall' together, so to speak. He discharged himself before completing his treatment and she left nursing and they set up home together and eventually got married and had children. A smiling Irish girl called Kathy also worked on the orthopaedic ward. She was a happy go lucky soul and became a friend of mine.

That summer Anne made me a fabulous black taffeta evening skirt, covered with black net and sequins, for dancing; with it I wore pretty blouses and silver dancing shoes; in the late autumn and winter I attended the ball in Hendon Police College and several hospital dances in the area during the festive season. These dances never ended before midnight or even later. Occasionally I did not get to bed until Iam. Yet I was often on duty by 8am next day. Vera and Bert came to the dances, too, and sometimes my friend Kathy was there as well. Nurses' pay was poor and these events were free and there was always company to get back to the nurses' home by bus or train, no matter what the hour.

LONDON, WINTER OF 1952

The author Charles Dickens vividly describes the London fog in the winters of the nineteenth century; in the twentieth century, because houses were heated by coal fires, fog caused by smoke emanating from countless chimney pots continued to descend on London every winter. At the beginning of December that particular winter the weather turned exceptionally cold and people burned even more coal than usual and supplemented it with wood, which caused yet more smoke. Steam trains were also run on coal, and that year buses changed to diesel oil, instead of petrol, which add-

Me with nursing colleague Lynn.

ed to the polluted atmosphere.

Inevitably, for about five days in early December a dense fog, like pea soup, descended on London and its suburbs; this period became known as the Great Smog of 1952, so called because of the soot content which gave the fog a yellow-black colour and a smell which pervaded all the senses: even theatres and cinemas closed because smog penetrated the auditoriums. Car headlights and torches were useless in penetrating it and everyone including dogs wore masks or thick scarves when they went out and about, and clothes became covered in grime and tar.

One day as I walked from home to Burnt Oak tube station to get to the hospital I could scarcely see my feet or my hands at arms' length as I crossed the Edgware Road, which was rather risky because trolley buses connected to overhead cables, though unseen, were still able to move very slowly.

Ward windows normally open day and night had to be shut and patients' beds on balconies moved to day rooms, while thousands of Londoners died from bronchial infections in a very short space of time, including some at our hospital. All the deaths kept florists and undertakers busy. It was obvious that smog was extremely detrimental to health. One afternoon as I made my way to Vera and Bert's home near Burnt Oak tube station, the smog was so dense I had to turn back and went to bed immediately I reached the nurses' home.

A week later the weather improved and I continued to work hard and study for exams but somehow I always found time and energy to go dancing. At each hospital dance I met Dr Trenchard, the consultant chest physician who had taken care of both Terry and me since our early teens, for he and his wife enjoyed

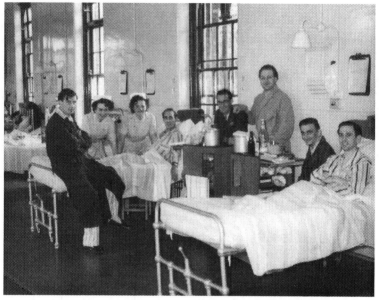

Me on the left, working on ward five at Colindale hospital.

dancing. To encourage people to mix there is a particular dance called the Paul Jones in which men and women face each other and move round to the music in opposite circles and when the music stops, they dance with whomever is facing them. As luck would have it, one night he became my dancing partner and as we waltzed around the ballroom he asked me 'Do you go dancing every night of your life?' I laughed as he suggested I should take more care of myself.

That Christmas Eve with friends from the nurses' home I took communion at the Colindale parish church and met Sister Bowyer among the congregation. I worked on Christmas Day and during the afternoon toured other wards with my friend Avril Duran who had a room adjoining mine in the Nurses' Home. She asked me to

Me, in the grounds of Colindale hospital where I have become a patient.

accompany her to the orthopaedic ward to see her favourite patient, David Sinclair. Like so many others she was crazy about him. We found him in bed, looking ill and bad tempered. He was not in the least pleased to see either of us, so we only stayed a minute or two and as we left the ward an elderly staff nurse there sang the song, 'Shrimp Boats Are a Coming' in a quavering voice, which we found highly amusing. I went home that night and on Boxing Day Dad decided to give a party for friends and neighbours. As usual by lunch time he had rolled back the dining room carpet ready for dancing and installed a barrel of beer in the hallway. All day he repeatedly played his favourite record, 'Christmas in Killarney with All the Folks at Home' which was very popular on the wireless

Ward six Christmas Day with Dr. Trenchard carving turkey.

that year. Now, if ever it is played I am reminded of him.

By mid evening the party was in full swing and everyone enjoyed themselves. Terry and I joined in until the early hours of the morning yet we never invited our friends, possibly due to the fact that none of us had any means of transport. Next day the four of us slept in till lunch time. Then I headed back to the nurses' home.

On New Year's Eve Dad invited our neighbours in for a drink and two of his cronies, barmen from The Flying Eagle in Mollison Way, turned up after the public house closed with an extension to 11pm. One of them, a wee Scotsman wearing the kilt, brought his wife along and the other was a bachelor, an attractive, silver tongued, powerfully built six foot four inch Irishman by the name of Johnny. They were both somewhat intoxicated on arrival and in the early hours of the morning they lost their temper with each other and started to fight. Dad managed to separate them and shut Johnny out in our back garden for a few minutes to cool off. At one point I thought we would have to call the police.

Later I helped Anne cook a sausage and bacon breakfast for guests still there and at dawn I stood at our front door and it started to snow as I waved good bye to the last of them

Only then, feeling very tired, did I go to bed. Terry had gone to bed early, though how he managed to get any sleep I do not know. Small wonder that a few weeks later I became ill and so did he.

CHAPTER TWENTY ONE

End of Nursing Career

Dad was never in the best of humour at the beginning of a new year. He always found it was a bleak time in the building trade with money in short supply, aggravated by the arrival of household bills. However, that January he did promise to make plans for my twenty first birthday in April and I drew up a list of twenty friends to be invited to a dinner party at a London hotel.

About four weeks later I woke up in the nurses home feeling as if I had influenza. After breakfast in the staff canteen I went on duty and my ward sister took one look at me and sent me to the sick bay. I was seen by a doctor, had a chest X-ray and a blood test and was confined to bed to await results. Alone, I passed the time reading a lot, and learnt two poems by heart, The Ancient Mariner and The Rubiyat of Omar Kyam.

Time passed and Professor Schnell, the senior consultant of the hospital, came to see me to confirm that I had tuberculosis. I was devastated and although I asked him how long it would take me to get well, I already knew the answer: at least three months in bed followed by another three months' recuperation: if I was lucky! I was moved to one of the women's wards and became a patient for the next sixteen months, missing my twenty first birthday party in April which would save Dad some money. I felt he would at least be glad about that.

Now I was the patient not the nurse and had to take the four-hourly intramuscular injections of Streptomycin and a liquid known as PAS at least twice daily, which I discovered had the most disgusting taste. Life was regimented by ward routine with a rest hour every day and lights went out at nine pm. We all had radio head sets connected to the Light Programme and Home Service until ten pm each day with half an hour extra on Saturday evening so that patients could listen to Saturday Night Theatre. There was also a hospital radio station which played patients' record requests every afternoon which were a comfort to me when I was alone during visiting hours. After a few weeks Dr. Trenchard gave me a minor operation called an artificial pneumothorax, when air is pumped into the space between lung and chest wall, to rest it, a procedure repeated every week to inhibit the lung's movement. Later I had the same treatment on my other lung.

On my twenty first birthday I was inundated with cards, telegrams, flowers and presents from my family, friends, patients and staff. Lizzie and Jim sent me a Bible, which I still have. Jim inscribed it. Now it is full of little mementoes of my life, some happy, like the receipt for the first night of my honeymoon at the Cumberland Hotel in London together with receipts for seats on the Paddington to Falmouth train the following day and cards from our son Malcolm and our little grand daughter, Lydia; and some sad, like the funeral service and cutting from the newspaper of the death of uncle Bill's grandson Terry Hill who was the first of the few British soldiers killed while driving an ambulance in the Gulf War of nineteen ninety one. Attending his funeral was a dramatic and harrowing experience.

On my birthday Winnie, who was my godmother, came to see me and gave me a poetry book, Palgraves Golden Treasury, and

George Borrow's Wild Wales. The patients of my former ward gave me a leather vanity case and manicure set, chocolates galore and flowers. One patient sent me a book of poems by Robert Herrick, which he inscribed with the kind words, 'Like crocus in the winter sun so is your smile. Like open sky to a frightened bird so is your sympathy'.

Several of my nursing friends from the Royal National Orthopaedic hospital sent gifts of crystal glass, books and pictures. But I have no recollection of a present from my Dad and Anne. They probably sent me flowers; and I never saw Terry. Years later he told me Dad forbade him to visit me for fear of catching tuberculosis. In those days, young people who were under the age of consent were more inclined to do as their parents ordered than they do in the twenty first century.

To help pass the time I joined a Book Club and received and read the novels of Neville Shute, Ernest Hemingway, Graham Greene and Somerset Maughan among others. I read all the classics in the hospital library: like the Brontë sisters, Jane Austen, Thomas Hardy, Leo Tolstoi, Honoré de Balzac and Oscar Wilde. However I never liked reading Shakespeare. I did a correspondence course in English literature paid for by the hospital, but I have forgotten it all, and I learnt to play chess with the patient in the next bed who was an actress called Sybil Ewbank. We became firm friends. At twenty five, her voice sounded just like her aunt's, the great Sybil Thorndyke, who, Sybil told me, had played Saint Joan in Bernard Shaw's play on the London stage in the nineteen thirties. She had many theatrical visitors, including her famous aunt, who became a Dame.

I did a lot of knitting and crosswords, made lampshades, and a tapestry which is still unfinished. I wrote many letters to friends and family, including a regular correspondence with cousin John who was still in the RAF. A few years later John left the services, so that he could go to University and become a science teacher. In this twenty first century we email each other.

CORONATION DAY

On 2nd June 1953 for seven hours the people of Great Britain were able to watch the whole of the Coronation of Queen Elizabeth the Second live on television which was most unusual. Nothing like it had ever happened before. After years of rationing and austerity it was a very big event and there was much excitement throughout the land which encouraged many people to go out and buy televisions and stay home for the day in order to watch it, sadly, only in black and white as colour television was not yet available.

Twelve inch televisions were installed in every ward in the hospital for patients and staff. The Royal Family were much admired: during the first half of the 20th century all over Great Britain audiences stood deferentially in theatres and concert halls while the National Anthem was played at the beginning of every performance. Likewise, in the cinema when the lights went up in the auditorium at the end of each day, before leaving, the audience stood still respectfully while it was played. Some time in the 1970s this practice ceased.

On Coronation day the weather was cold and in London it poured with rain all day long. In our ward, work was curtailed to allow staff time to view. Sybil and I and the other patients watched the whole event from our beds. The quality of reproduction was so poor that we had to draw the ward curtains to see it. My most distinct memory is seeing the Queen of Tonga sitting in an open carriage in the pouring rain. Terry remembers the day because he was working as a window dresser at the large London Co-operative Departmental Store in Burnt Oak where a television was installed for the staff.

By the beginning of summer I had put on weight and was allowed to get up and dress and walk about the hospital and grounds for two hours a day which made life more tolerable. In some ways the whole experience of being a patient with its restrictions and in my case, virtually no visitors except friends among the staff, was like being in prison.

In early August we were informed by our ward sister that a short technicolor film of the coronation would be shown that week to ambulant patients and hospital staff in the Memorial Hall beside the Nurses' Home.

There was a sense of excitement that afternoon as patients, some in wheel chairs, plus a number of hospital staff, gathered together in the hall. A hush descended on the audience as the film began, but as soon as the figure of our new Queen appeared on the screen in all her regalia, I heard a loud voice just behind me, with what at first I took to be a Canadian accent, declare 'This is not our Queen Elizabeth the Second. Queen Elizabeth the First of England had our Queen's head chopped off.' I realised at once it was a Scot speaking, for Queen Elizabeth the First had signed the death warrant of Mary Queen of Scots. I turned to discover it was none other than DAVID SINCLAIR, the idol of so many of my nursing friends, who used to glare at me over the top of his newspaper from his ward balcony as I had passed by on my way off duty. He was looking well, compared with his dreadful appearance when I had been persuaded by Avril to visit him last Christmas Day. Wheelchair bound, with the whole of his right leg encased in plaster, his hair was blonde and he looked handsome and sunburnt. Several times in the next few minutes he repeated his remarks loudly. I turned and glared at him. I understood his sentiments, but thought him very rude, for he was spoiling it for everyone else. Eventually other male patients managed to calm him down.

Unknown to me Terry, approaching nineteen year of age, began working in Queensbury at the chemist chain Timothy Whites and Dad continued to forbid him to visit me. On television from our ward beds in late August Sybil and I saw the England cricket team beat Australia and win the Ashes at the Oval with Don Bradman out for a duck in his last ever Test innings which reminded me of the day three years before when I was there with my friend Dossie.

In September I was allowed to get up, dress and walk about the hospital most of the day, often meeting male patients that I had nursed, several of whom came back to visit me when they were discharged fit. I enjoyed their visits tremendously because I seldom saw my family, most of whom lived too far away, or like Dad and Anne were too frightened to visit me.

BROADSTAIRS

One day Dad came to see me on his own to tell me he was planning to sell the house and move to Broadstairs in Kent. I was distressed at the news. It was true I seldom saw him but now I concluded I would be seeing even less of him. After his departure I fled to the washroom where I was comforted by fellow patients.

I remember one of them sat with me and gave me a cigarette, to console me. Patients were allowed to smoke when not in bed. How times have changed! A short time later, on his next visit, Dad was pleased to see me up and dressed and suggested I walk with him to one of the male wards to see a friend of his, a taxi driver who was a patient. Dad told him of his plans to move house and his friend could not believe it, saying. 'Bill, why are you making arrangements to move while Kathleen is still a patient here?' Dad did not reply. Perhaps he thought I was about to be discharged from the hospital.

I continued to take daily medication and injections, with x-rays and blood tests every month and I was allowed to dress and stay up all day long and at the end of August 1953 I was made chairman of my ward. Chairmen met once a month in the Memorial Hall, to discuss how to provide entertainment for fellow patients, some of whom were confined to bed for two or more years.

When I went along to a committee meeting I was horrified to find David Sinclair in charge of the proceedings. I can still recall the pompous look he gave me when he saw me enter the hall. I decided I had never met anyone so arrogant. He made it extremely plain he disliked me just as much as I did him! Yet I must confess I liked his attractive Scottish accent, broad shoulders and blonde good looks, and was disturbed by his penetrating grey eyes and very long lashes!

HEAD OVER HEELS

We managed to control our animosity sufficiently to discuss with others improvements in our facilities, like the radio record request programme run by and for patients, with plans to broadcast it most of the day, plus more frequent whist drives and plans too, for quiz games broadcast in the afternoons with teams of patients. Already I enjoyed going to whist drives and every ward had an occasional film. After the success of the Coronation film held in the Community Hall we sought and were given permission for films for patients to be shown there once a fortnight in the early evening,

With two other female patients, I attended the first one but I remember nothing of it. It must have been a poor film for the attendance that evening was very low and chairs for about a dozen patients were put up on the stage behind the curtain. It was very dark when we arrived and the film had just begun as we found our seats. Sitting there I had my hands looped round the back of my chair and in the middle of the film I was suddenly aware of a hand holding mine, and that now familiar Scottish voice whispering 'Kathy, I adore you.' It was, of course David Sinclair. I had not realised he was there. Would you believe it? I just fell head over heels in love. I still cannot understand why!

Afterwards, as we all headed back to our wards I noticed he was walking with the aid of a stick with a smaller plaster on his leg. I arrived at my ward in a trance! Sybil was sitting up in bed waiting to hear about the film, but all I could say was 'I don't remember it. I think I have fallen in love with............ David Sinclair.'

She said 'You must be mad, you dislike each other!' Not any more! I could not sleep that night, for thinking of him and his hand in mine. Next day I received my first love letter from him and we began a daily correspondence, with staff passing letters between us.

We were fortunate that ambulant patients had a certain amount of freedom within the hospital grounds which enabled David and me to meet every day, and he introduced me to his special friend and fellow patient, Johnny Withey. They were running the hospital radio together but quite how they managed it I do not know because they spent so much time laughing. They liked playing their favourite tunes, and David used every opportunity to play the records of Benny Goodman, his favourite musician and Johnny was nuts about the American singer Johnny Ray whose most popular song began 'If your sweetheart sends a letter of goodbye, it's no secret you'll feel better if you cry'.

We requested romantic love songs to be played for each other and a favourite of mine was Doris Day singing Secret Love. I did not know then that she was David's favourite film star. David's fellow patients Olie, Brian Webster and Ronny Bureen sent in record requests for us, too. As a consequence even now many years later all the romantic melodies of the forties and fifties take us back to those days when we first fell in love.

The Patients' Committee set up a programme based on a BBC radio panel game of the time called Twenty Questions with David as Chairman and Johnny and me among the panel members. We met every morning for rehearsals, and had a lot of fun. David and Johnny always joked a lot. I wish I could remember the funny satirical things that David said which had us all in stitches; with each succeeding day we were more in love. It was a wonderful feeling. At the same time Johnny, too, was in love. He had found himself a girl friend among the hospital staff. She was the Irish girl, Kathy, with whom I had worked. It was a happy time for all four of us. Years later Kathy told me that staff turned a blind eye when she visited him in his ward and she had been known to stay after the visiting hour and then had to climb out through the window in the sluice room just in case a nurse would report her for fraternising with a patient. While all this was happening I weighed nine stone, with a narrow waist and a forty two inch bust!! I felt well. How wrong I was.

For in late September I received a shock when Dr. Schnell called me to his office and gave me an ultimatum, two more years on bed rest, or thoracic surgery involving two operations for the removal of part of one lung, with recuperation in six months. I was given 24 hours to decide which to go for. I opted for surgery.

SURGERY

Mr Jackson, the surgeon with whom I had worked in theatre, came to see me. Distressed to meet me as a patient, he remembered how he had once joked about giving me a thoracoplasty and apologised profusely saying he much regretted it and would never do such a thing again. He suggested the unusual step of giving me a general anaesthetic. I accepted his offer, though normally operations were carried out under a local anaesthetic.

On Sunday 4th Oct. 1953 I moved across to a side room of a male medical ward where only a year before I had worked for a time. That evening, wearing a thick maroon winter dressing gown to keep out the chilly night air, I stepped out into the long hospital corridor to watch my Dad go home, knowing that the following morning I would be in theatre under Mr. Jackson's knife! Suddenly, as if from nowhere David appeared at my side. He too had been watching his visitor depart. We were drawn together, and he quietly told me he loved me. Despite knowing I had to face major surgery next morning, at that moment I was in Seventh Heaven.

Next day Mr. Jackson successfully removed a lobe of my left lung. David was allowed to visit me in the side ward and I vaguely recall Dad and Anne's presence. A week later, after several painful and uncomfortable days, Mr. Jackson performed a second operation called a plombage, which involved installing a number of light weight plastic balls within a net, placed in the space where the lobe of my lung had been. However, within twenty four hours I began to develop a high fever and at times I was delirious, cause unknown. It was decided I needed a lumbar puncture to ascertain why. Early that afternoon I remember climbing up in bed to reach the thermometer on the wall above and taking my own temperature which was 105.8 degrees. Shortly afterwards I had to show a staff nurse called Norma just how to place the equipment for a lumbar puncture for she hadn't a clue what to do.

The result was that I had an acute streptococcal infection, requiring an immediate operation to remove the plombage together with several ribs so that my chest wall would fall in and fill the space where my lung had been. I was too ill to sign my own consent form, and my Dad could not be contacted. Terry told me years later that Dr. Trenchard phoned him at work and said the operation was so urgent that he could sign on my behalf. Quite how this would be allowed I do not know because in those days the age of consent was twenty one. However, Dad did turn up at the hospital just in time and was extremely angry on seeing Terry until he was informed why he was there.

Before the operation I have a vague recollection of Dad and Anne's presence. She was mopping my brow and at 9.30pm that night as I travelled to the theatre on a hospital trolley, I caught a glimpse of a lone figure standing in the gloomy corridor. I did not know then that it was David. He told me, months later, that one of my colleagues had told him what was happening to me. Somehow he had managed to leave his ward in hopes of seeing me and prayed for me as I passed by. His prayers were answered for the operation was a success.

RECOVERY

For a month I recuperated in that side ward, with a course of antibiotics and intensive physiotherapy. David was allowed to visit me every day, sitting beside me holding my hand, the best medicine in the world. We talked endlessly and told each other about our families, and once he showed me a photograph of his little sister Madeleine and told me that his ambition was to become a newspaper reporter: when he first came to London at the age of sixteen before he was taken ill he had worked for a short time at the Daily Telegraph.

David's friend Johnny was declared fit and left the hospital: we heard that he married Kathy by special licence on the 31st October.

Even though David visited me every afternoon as soon as I was able we exchanged long letters; and at last he was free of plaster casts and learning to walk without a crutch. One day, I was delighted to see Terry who came to see me on his bicycle. I had missed him a lot.

David wanted to send me some red roses and asked the mother of Brian Baxter, a fellow patient, if she could arrange it. However it was not the season for roses so the following day Mrs Baxter brought me some michaelmas daisies from her garden and put them in a vase on my bedside table, saying they were with love from David. He came in later, and as soon as he saw them he wanted to know who had given me 'weeds', and I never received any roses. Ever since, in the month of October if we see them in people's gardens I remind him.

I first met my future mother in law Florence Ellen Sinclair when she came to my side ward looking for her son. Slim, of average height with grey eyes and blonde hair, she looked distressed and weary because, the day before, a spark from a coal fire in her living room had ignited the carpet and partially destroyed her flat, but she said that David's little sister Madeleine was safe because she had been at school when it happened.

In November after four weeks in the side ward I returned to the female ward, somewhat slimmer than when I had left it. In less than four weeks my bust had shrunk from 42 inches to 34 inches! Now I had to conform to official visiting hours and David, a male patient, was forbidden to visit me at all. We continued to write long loving letters to each other every day, delivered by our friends, and from my ward window I caught an occasional glimpse of him standing on his ward balcony.

I wrote and told auntie Lizzie that I hoped to marry him one day. She did not live long enough to meet him but he loved her sisters and in future years whenever we went to visit them, if he found them together, he affectionately described them as 'The Taffia'.

Uncle Tom visited me, and spent a couple of hours at my bedside telling me about life in the Fleet Air Arm during the war years and the fun he had in America at the end of hostilities and how, after the war he had wanted to emigrate to Australia with his family. I am very glad they did not do so.

Just before Christmas 1953 David was walking quite well and

declared fit and discharged from the hospital with a slight limp, which meant he could come and see me in visiting hours. Terry, whom I seldom saw, had begun working at an estate agency in Cricklewood. He had a girl friend called Marion whom he brought to see me that Christmas and they took David home with them to Raeburn Road to meet Dad and Anne. Visitors were allowed for several hours on Christmas Day 1953 and David was with me most of the time and we sat in the corner of my little ward locked in an embrace! My present to him was a voucher to buy a record. I remember writing 'Buy anything you like, but not a Benny Goodman record,' because I could not understand his music and it was not suitable for ballroom dancing!

David knew I liked poetry and gave me the Works of Lord Byron. I still have this book, with a loving inscription from him and of course, he bought himself a Benny Goodman record!

Regulations were relaxed during the festive season and on Boxing Day several of my former patients came in to see me during the evening, a great end to a lovely Christmas. A few days later David showed me a chrome cigarette case with a map of Great Britain on it, which was a present given him by Terry's girl friend. It made me very jealous! In those days most adults smoked cigarettes, including David and me.

1954

In the spring Terry came to see me and told me he was taking a job window dressing at Timothy Whites in Devon. By that time I was well on the way to a complete recovery and Dad and Anne had moved from Raeburn Road to a new detached house, designed to his specifications, at St Peters, Broadstairs in Kent, with the hope that both Terry and I would join them there later in the year. Meanwhile I was allowed out of the hospital confines for increasing periods of time which gave me a sense of euphoria and a feeling as if I had been released from prison. I went shopping for fashionable clothes in Edgware and spent every minute I could with David.

I was allowed leave to spend Easter with him and his family in their flat at Abbey Road, sharing a bedroom with his twelve year old sister Madeleine, a little girl with long golden plaits. David and I gave each other boxed Sweetheart Easter cards, which intrigued her so much that to hide his embarrassment, he sat on his card most of the weekend. Feeling radiant with happiness early on Easter Saturday morning, I went with her on a bus to the local newsagent and when we returned she announced that all the male passengers on the bus kept looking at me. It was probably because I could not stop smiling.

On Easter Sunday morning, Ferg, David's dear mother's partner, escorted me to morning service at Hampstead parish church and when we returned David was shamefaced because he had not come with us. It was my birthday that weekend and Madeleine made me a birthday cake, with one huge wax candle in the middle! It tasted awful, but we all ate a slice to please her.

David's mother asked me to call her Florrie, but I was too shy and after a couple more visits to their home, she told him she thought I didn't like her, which wasn't true. So the very next time when we were doing the washing up together in her little kitchen I plucked up courage and called her Florrie. From that day on it was easy, and we became friends. On 10th May that year I was discharged from Colindale hospital and the feeling was absolutely incredible. I felt like a bird let out of a cage. The theatre sister of the hospital came to see me before I left and suggested I could become a dental nurse or a medical secretary.

FRINTON ON SEA

With fifteen other women from different hospitals in the London area the NHS sent me by train for two weeks' convalescence to Frinton on Sea, Essex, staying at a large black and white three storey detached Victorian house on the sea front. I had been there four years before, recovering from minor surgery, so it was already familiar to me.

British people did not go abroad much in the early nineteen fifties and package holidays were unheard of. Frinton was, and possibly still is, a very select seaside resort, famous then for its wealthy holiday makers, bracing east coast air and beautiful greensward fronting several very large hotels along the cliff top: at the foot of the cliffs, reached by a zig zag path, were lots of colourful seaside chalets, a shingle beach and sea breakers, but there was not a single council deck chair in sight. Far too posh!

There were no public houses in the town and day trippers and coach parties were banned. The town clock was switched off at 11pm every night so that residents and holiday makers alike could sleep peacefully in their beds and the milkman was not allowed to make any deliveries before 7am. It was a lovely resort. Fifty years later in the twenty first century I heard it announced on the radio that Frinton town council have at last agreed to the erection of the town's first public house.

One day while I was staying there the fire brigade called. The property we were staying in had no fire escape and they wished to demonstrate a new device they had to help people trapped in a fire. We all trooped up to the top of the house and I volunteered to be their guinea pig. The firemen placed some straps around me and I climbed out onto the parapet and absailed down the building. I am normally frightened of heights, but somehow it did not bother me that day, and I enjoyed the experience.

David and I wrote to each other every day while I was there and though we were apart the love songs on the radio helped to console me. He gave me the surprising news that Kathy had given birth to a baby girl called Geraldine. I spent some of my savings buying clothes, including a green Dannimac and a navy blue spotted tie for David and a pretty scarf for his mother.

CHAPTER TWENTY TWO

After Nursing

I had been in Frinton almost two weeks when I received a telegram from Addie to say Lizzie was very ill in Morriston Hospital, Swansea. I sent Terry a telegram, rang David's mother at her office and left Frinton for London the following day en route for Wales. David met me off the train looking very handsome in a new navy blazer and grey slacks. It was magic to be together again. I stayed one night with him and his family and then with a heavy heart I took the train to Burry Port.

After six years away I found little change in the town. Station Road was exactly as I had known it but when I began to walk up the tram way I found it had been replaced with a children's playground and there was a country park where some of farmer Edwards' fields used to be, through which I walked to reach Colby Road. The lane to Rhandir Delyn was just as stony and rocky as ever it had been and both house and garden had a thoroughly neglected air. Addie, little Bobbie and Mary greeted me at the front door and uncle Jim looked very frail, confused and totally lost without Lizzie.

I slept in what used to be Terry's bedroom and next day by the time I got to Lizzie's bedside at the hospital with Mary, she had slipped into a coma from which she never recovered, and she died that night. Terry sent a telegram to say he was unable to come to Wales. Neither I nor anyone else knew the reason was that he didn't have enough money. Communications were slow in those days as very few people had access to a telephone.

Next day Addie and I took the bus to Llanelly, where she bought me a black and white tweed coat and I bought myself a small black velvet hat and gloves. Lizzie's funeral took place in early June and as we followed the funeral cortege into St Mary's the church drive was lined with members of the Towns Women's Guild and the nave was full of her friends, with the family at the front. Most of her brothers and sisters were present: I especially remember Charlie because he was so upset. I was not physically fit enough to remain in Burry Port to look after Jim or visit my old school friends but I waited until his doctor had made arrangements for a nurse to call regularly to attend to him, and Addie remained there with Bobbie, to look after him for a while.

Mary and I were met at Paddington station by David and his sister Madeleine. Mary went on to Margate and I stayed with David and his family and he helped me find a bed sitting room, with the use of a kitchen, on the ground floor at the front of an Edwardian house run by two ladies in Swiss Cottage. For four weeks, before looking for employment, we spent most of our waking hours together and truly got to know each other well. Like most people in London we travelled everywhere by bus or the London Underground, sitting in little cafés, coffee shops or the back row of cinemas in and around Hampstead. Our favourite cinema was the Swiss Cottage Odeon where a bus stopped right outside. On sunny afternoons we enjoyed walking together in Regent's Park and I adored dressing up to go and meet him, feeling that all the popular romantic songs of the day had been written especially for us. A highlight was going to the Duke of York's Theatre to see The Confidential Clerk, with Denholm Elliott. I cannot remember a thing about it, now, but at the time it was wonderful.

Florrie was a telephonist at Sumlock, in the City of London, and her company offered David a job in their accounts department. He took it, and I was accepted as a trainee dental nurse in Cricklewood and worked there for three months.

TERRY

To my surprise on the Saturday of the August Bank holiday, held at the beginning of the month in those days, my landladies called me to the phone in their room because Terry was on the line. He had just got off the train from Plymouth and told me he was on his way to Broadstairs to see Dad and Anne. We arranged to meet at Swiss Cottage Underground station and I quickly dressed and left the house wearing the latest fashion - flat white leather shoes and black figure-hugging sweater with a tightly fitted knee length black and white fine check skirt. When he saw me he did not recognise me and whistled, because, he said, I looked stunning! That's my brother!

He was starving hungry so we bought food and I took him back to my bedsit and we talked while eating, then we travelled by the Underground to Victoria station which was absolutely packed with holiday makers queuing at all platform entrances. No motor ways and fewer cars in the fifties meant most people stayed in Great Britain and travelled by train on their holidays. I stayed with Terry until he boarded a train to Broadstairs.

I spent the Bank holiday with David and his family in Abbey Road, and his mother invited me to go and live with them in a large Victorian house called St John's Lodge in Swiss Cottage where they were about to take a lease on a garden flat, with its own entrance.

This lovely house has since been demolished and replaced with an extremely nondescript block of flats.

ST PETERS

Before moving in David and I spent a weekend with Dad and Anne at their new house in Broadstairs, travelling down by train from Victoria on a Friday evening. We were met by Dad at the station in his 1937 Austin Seven coupé with a new engine.

My heart warmed at the sight of him and he greeted us with the words 'The weather is wonderful, it never rains in Broadstairs!' and we tried not to laugh because Kent was known as The Garden of England, and all gardens need rain.

He was so proud of his four bed roomed detached house at the bottom of a small culdesac in St Peters, fifteen minutes walk from Broadstairs sea front, designed exactly as he wanted, and it had that lovely new smell. It was centrally heated; he had decorated all the interior himself; the furnishing were new except for the three piece suite from our home in Edgware, re-covered in a maroon uncut moquette and backed with lace antimacassars. It was standing on an ice-blue carpet in what Dad called the lounge, with a fire place, wall lights, coffee table and television.

The dining room included two Cintique armchairs either side of a tiled fireplace with a French window looking out onto a sizeable back garden; there was a hatch through to the kitchen, which had fitted cupboards and a cooker with a bell on it. But there was only one loo which was upstairs beside the bathroom.

I was on tenterhooks the whole time we were there, because Dad made me feel as if we were at the Ideal Home Exhibition. Always an early riser and first up, when he was not working he expected everyone else to get up early too. A favourite way he achieved this was by turning up the volume of the radio, making it impossible to sleep and calling out 'It is a beautiful morning, breakfast is served.' So, knowing him well, I rose early and called David to get up.

Anne worked as manageress of a Broadstairs department store and when she had gone that Saturday morning, David and I sat in the dining room on the Cintique armchairs (backed with lacy antimacassars) and talked with Dad who eventually made a pot of tea and as he passed David a cup, I was dumbfounded to hear him say 'David, be careful not to put your head on the antimacassar in case it gets marked.'

David's reply was, 'Michael, it's there for that purpose, to protect the chair!' It was the fashion for men to use brylcreem on their hair and the irony was that both Dad and David used it.

Broadstairs was an attractive resort full of old world charm, much of which is still retained fifty years later. We enjoyed exploring on foot, dreaming of the day when we would be married, living in a nice house with a Sunbeam Talbot car in the drive. We walked down to the sea through the narrow York Gate, past an old pub called the Tartar Frigate, beside a sandy bay and the attractive harbour where little boats were moored; and on the cliff top, above, we saw Bleak House, where Charles Dickens had lived for a short period; and we found a delicious ice cream bar.

That Saturday night we dined at home on a polished table with table mats, place settings and damask table napkins. While Anne was still eating, for she loved to finish her dinner with cheese, Dad served coffee. Unfortunately David had the effrontery to light a cigarette without asking. Although they were both heavy smokers,

I could see from the looks passed between them that they did not approve of his behaviour and I quickly suggested we take our coffee and go and sit in the lounge. However this did not go down well either, because Dad feared we would spill our coffee on his ice-blue carpet! All in all, it was a tense time within the house, making me a bag of nerves.

However, when he was behind the wheel of his car Dad was a different person, less domineering and quite charming. On Sunday morning, in his little jalopy with the hood down, we were taken round the country lanes watching rabbits at play in the fields and admiring the sea views and pretty villages, and ending up beside the very atmospheric Tartar Frigate pub on Broadstairs sea front where Dad bought a round of drinks. There were no drink and drive laws, little traffic and he knew the area well.

On our return to London, I moved in to the large garden flat at St John's Lodge with David and his family. The front door led to a central hall, containing a coal stove which heated the flat in winter, with all rooms leading off: there were three bedrooms, a bathroom and a separate loo, a large kitchen and a beautiful lounge with a piano. I shared a bedroom with Madeleine who started attending the local comprehensive school and in a very short while I taught her to sleep with the bedroom fanlights open. She still likes an open bedroom window, even in the depth of winter.

I gave up training to be a dental nurse and at the start of the autumn term I enrolled as a full time student studying Gregg shorthand and typing at a college in Swiss Cottage and David attended evening classes there. He still hankered to be a reporter and thought shorthand would help him achieve his ambition.

At half term Florrie gave Madeleine a budgerigar, and I took her by train and bus to Hanwell to visit auntie Addie who had returned from looking after uncle Jim in Burry Port. Addie told me that now that the summer season was over Mary had left little Clive with Jim in Margate, and taking Michael with her had gone down to Burry Port to see uncle Jim Ogborn.

Mary wrote and told me that on arrival at Rhandir Delyn she discovered he was very ill and arranged for a doctor to call and get Jim transferred to hospital where he died the following day. She said that the vicar of St Mary's called at the house as Jim was leaving in the ambulance and that she had asked the vicar why parishioners had not been more supportive after all the good work both he and Lizzie had done in the parish over the years. The vicar replied that the lane leading to Rhandir Delyn was very rocky and difficult for people to walk up. Aunty Mary quickly retorted that it was also a rocky road to Calvary but it did not stop Jesus when he carried his Cross. I think her words struck home. Meanwhile Gran Hill was being cared for in hospital, where she had been for some time and sadly I could not afford the money to attend Jim's funeral.

Johnny and Kathy, with baby Geraldine, were living in Kingsbury with his father, and David and I had lots of fun with them going to jazz concerts on Sunday afternoons in local cinemas. I recall seeing John Dankworth and his band at the Harrow Odeon where each section of musicians wore different colour suits and stood up in unison when playing. At the Savoy cinema in Burnt Oak we saw the drummer Alan Ganley with tall handsome Jack Parnell and his band and were very impressed with the two-drum finale. One afternoon we all went to see ex-patient Ronnie Bureen whose mother gave us a wonderful tea party and as we sat round the dining table to eat it we all started laughing for no particular reason and just could not stop. We became quite hysterical. I do not remember ever laughing so much in all my life.

COLLEGE

I enjoyed being 'back at school' very much but I was not a born typist, for I was too slow. I made a friend there called Jill Charles, a state registered nurse, trained at Kings College hospital, who commuted from Walton on Thames on a Vespa motor bike. Traffic was light and there were few cars along the Finchley Road then. It has changed a great deal. Students congregated for lunch at a local café in Swiss Cottage where we discussed either the latest television programme which everyone saw as there were only two channels, or the latest Goon Show episode, a radio programme, all the rage at the time with Peter Sellers, Spike Milligan and Harry Secombe. Once I sat on the back of Jill's Vespa and we spent the lunch hour in Regents Park. I stayed for a couple of weekends at her home in Walton on Thames where her parents lived in rural splendour and were as delightful as she was. Oh! how I wish I had kept in touch.

Florrie took two weeks' sick leave that autumn during which time I got up early and made breakfast for us all before attending the college and discovered David was morose at that time of day. He hardly spoke a word before leaving for work and Florrie found me in tears after he had gone and explained 'You will have to get used to what is a family trait,' and then she went on to explain that though they travelled to work together on the Underground they never spoke to each other until they reached the Sumlock office. What was marvellous about having her at home was that when I returned from college she would have a cup of tea and a cigarette ready for me and we had a few minutes to ourselves before Mando returned from school. I loved her for it and I thought her motherly.

With Addie and Bobbie home from Burry Port, David and I enjoyed many visits to their home in Hanwell. We also visited Winnie, Arthur and the children. As we walked through a pathway near Colindale hospital on our first visit to reach their home we got soaked in a rainstorm but we didn't care a scrap. We were just happy to be well and free.

ARSENAL FOOTBALL MATCH

All his life David had been a football supporter of Heart of Midlothian, an Edinburgh football team known as Hearts, Jam Tarts or Jambos. So when one Saturday that autumn my uncle Tom invited us to join him and his friends standing behind the Arsenal goal at Highbury in north London to watch a match David was delighted. It was the first professional football match I ever saw and I will always remember it because just before half time I fainted, probably due to the fact that we had eaten very little and it was a bitterly cold day. I was lifted over the heads of spectators to the touch line, to be treated by St John's Ambulance Brigade. My anxious uncle accompanied me but my loving would-be fiancé stayed to watch the match and to find out if he had won the raffle then going on amongst the group of spectators we were with! Finance obviously was more important than love, although he did in fact win the raffle!

When I had recovered Tom and I spent the rest of the match sitting comfortably on the touch line, and afterwards, as we made our way to the station, by chance we met my uncle Harry who had been sitting in the stand. He laughed when he was told it was me that had fainted and we joined him for a cup of tea at a café. The whole time he insisted on calling David 'Jock' because of his pronounced Scottish accent. Now, however, David sounds as though he has lived in Surrey all his life, except when he speaks to a fellow Scot, or we go north of the Border, when miraculously his accent returns!

SWINGING LONDON

With our friends, especially Brian Baxter, whenever we could afford it we attended jazz concerts: at the Albert Hall where we saw the Ted Heath Band, Sarah Vaughan and the Mills Brothers; at Earls Court Louis Armstrong; at The Hundred Club in Oxford Street Humphrey Lyttleton and his band, where the cellar was so packed with people I had to sit on the stage beneath Humph as he played his trumpet. We saw the excellent bands of Ronnie Scott and Dave Brubeck at the Dominion in Tottenham Court Road. Tubby Hayes is a musician I will never forget, for his saxophone playing was superb and while listening to drummer Tony Crombie and his band at the Gaumont State I needed ear plugs. Brian was friendly with guitarist Bert Weedon and after a performance we went on stage and Brian introduced us to him. The most unusual concert we attended was given by the Modern Jazz Quartet where the whole audience, including David, sat silent and still which astounded me. I decided then I did not enjoy listening to them, yet many years later I learnt to appreciate their style.

Occasionally David and I went to the theatre in London. I recall seeing the play The Mousetrap, still running fifty years later. Once, with Johnny and Kathy, we queued for over an hour at the

Essoldo cinema in Kilburn High Road to see the film Seven Brides for Seven Brothers, but did not succeed in getting in, so we went window shopping along the street instead, for in those days it was a good shopping centre.

One evening we went with Florrie and Ferg to a BBC broadcast of Edmundo Ross and his Latin American Band, in a studio somewhere in Oxford Street, I sat in the auditorium and watched David dance the Samba with his mother, which they both enjoyed tremendously.

THE HONEY POT INN

My nursing friend Vera and her husband Bert still lived in Burnt Oak. Vera had an unattached brother, a sergeant in the South Wales Borderers, stationed somewhere in the locality, who often visited them and for a period of time David and I congregated at Vera's home on Saturday evenings before we all made our way by bus to the Honey Pot public house in Queensbury, where music was played in the saloon bar by a guitarist and a pianist, two quite talented Latin American musicians. Vera's brother, wearing his army dress uniform, frequently came with us. I liked him, but if he so much as looked at me, I could sense David wanted to cleave him in two!

Customers at the Honey Pot were encouraged by the musicians to get up and sing with the aid of a microphone. David was a favourite, singing the popular songs of the time, Nature Boy, Stranger in Paradise, Autumn Leaves and September in the Rain, while Vera's brother was great at singing traditional airs. We needed to be there early to get good seats and the atmosphere was very convivial.

Johnny and Kathy sometimes joined us there when they could

get a baby sitter. Once, when David started to sing, Kathy was sitting contentedly listening, but Johnny and I for no particular reason were suddenly convulsed in laughter and had to hide our heads under a table until David had finished singing.

That winter I knitted David a long sleeved woollen cricket sweater. Although it was much too big he wore it with pride for a very short while. Once! Winnie, Arthur and my cousins Ronald and Linda spent that Christmas with Dad and Anne; and Terry invited his girlfriend from Edgware to join them. But I stayed in London with David and his family and we celebrated at St John's Lodge where I recall helping to stuff a goose, make mince pies and listening to Florrie playing Chopin and boogie woogie on the piano and dancing the eightsome reel in the lounge on New Year's Eve.

THE YEAR 1955

In the New Year David completed his shorthand and typing course but did not become a newspaper reporter. Instead he became a cost accountant at Vintens, a factory manufacturing underwater cameras on the North Circular Road, near Staples Corner. There he met a fellow Scot, Jock Lewis, and they became friends. I left Gregg's College and did shorthand and typing for the Brook Street Bureau who specialised in temporary secretarial work in London's West End; after a few weeks I ended up as a temporary secretary at the British Medical Association, known as the BMA, where I spent some months typing stencils for the British Dental Association.

At home Florrie announced we would all have to look for fresh accommodation as the lease on St. John's Lodge was about to expire and she had plans to move to Earls Court. However, David decided to stay in Swiss Cottage and share a flat with Jock in a large Edwardian terrace house in Fellows Road and Johnny and Kathy gave me a home with them in Kingsbury until I found a place to live near David. I commuted via the Underground to Euston and walked along to the BMA. Johnny's suburban home reminded me of my parents' house in nearby Edgware. Kathy was a housewife looking after baby Geraldine and David and I spent happy evenings with them there at The Plough public house watching Johnny and David play bar billiards.

Despite some misgivings about another trip to Broadstairs, on Maundy Thursday, wearing court shoes with extremely high heels and a cream suit, I met David at Victoria station and we spent Easter with Dad and Anne. In February Terry had been sent to a sanatorium at Lenham in Kent and on Easter Sunday we all visited him and he told me he had fallen in love with a girl from Broadstairs called Joan Swan. She worked as a librarian in the town and he became so enamoured of her that he kept borrowing books every day just to see her. She was not very tall so he liked to get her to climb the step ladder for a book just so that he could see her legs! She was in love with him and visited him every week. In June he was transferred to Grove Park Hospital in London, where he had a lobe of his left lung removed. Joan took a job in the book section of a large department store called Bourne and Hollingsworth in London's Oxford Street so that she could be near him.

That summer I found myself a bedsit in Belsize Park with a french window giving access to a walled garden, and after a further period doing stencils at the BMA I left the Brook Street Bureau and started working for a local dentist. At weekends when we were not visiting my aunts and our families David and I began visiting

Lords regularly to watch Middlesex play cricket, and once when we were travelling there by bus a stranger gave us his tickets for the Members' Enclosure.

In the house where David and Jock lived we made friends with a young couple, Ken and Pauline, who travelled about on a motor bike and eventually married and left Swiss Cottage to work for the forestry commission in central Wales; there was a Rumanian, called Gregor, who played guitar and was seldom in this world - years later we realised he must have been on drugs - and there was Sandy, who lived in a studio flat at the top of a house on the opposite side of Fellows Road: whenever we visited him he insisted we remove our shoes and put yellow dusters on our feet to prevent marking his polished floors! He was an artist and a closet homosexual: we all knew it and liked him. He asked us all to go with him to the local health centre, to see a special viewing of a film about the atomic bomb on Hiroshima but I was the only one who could face it. We also made friends with a couple, husband and wife Malcolm and Helen Ross, who had two little children and lived in a flat at Primrose Hill. Malcolm was the manager of Boyds piano shop in Watford and Helen was a delightful Frenchwoman. They often invited us to dinner and she cooked the most wonderful tomato omelettes, using nine eggs for the four of us, washed down with French wine. Delicious!

Determined to get me to like the music of his favourite musician, David took me to see the film The Benny Goodman Story at the Dominion in Tottenham Court Road and we sat through it twice. In all we saw the film at least half a dozen more times, just for the pleasure of listening to him and his music and I am now a Benny Goodman fan. I wanted David to like the music of Beethoven too and I persuaded him to take me to a concert at the Royal Festival Hall where we had to stand and David leaned against a wall which turned out to be a door, through which he fell in the middle of the concert. When that happened, coupled with the fact that he thought Beethoven far too noisy, he was put off for life!

Terry and Joan got engaged a few days after his twenty first birthday in September, spent like mine as a patient in hospital. I did not realise they had waited until he had reached the age of consent because Dad disapproved of the match from the beginning. It took them nearly two years to save enough money to get married.

There were many little restaurants where we could buy a decent meal; and with or without our friends, on just one drink and a cigarette we spent many happy evenings in local public houses in Englands Lane or the Swiss Cottage Tavern on the Finchley Road, but of course as none of us had cars we would sometimes imbibe a little more. When Johnny and Kathy joined us he and David enjoyed a glass of brandy while Kathy and I were fond of a rum with black currant or coca cola, or just a glass of sherry. We had lots of simple fun and did not need to spend much money to enjoy ourselves. I am sure that Kathy could get drunk just by looking at a glass of sherry, she was such a happy soul. Malcolm and Helen gave wonderful parties in their flat on Primrose Hill: on New Year's Eve we were entertained well into the night by a classical guitarist and David got drunk on gin, vowing never to drink it again.

THE YEAR 1956

We celebrated David's birthday at Fellows Road with a party for friends and I gave him a bottle of ink with the most expensive pen manufactured at that time, called a Parker 51. He treasured it for more than twenty years until the day he gave it to our son Malcolm to use at school (and he lost it within a week without any appreciation of its sentimental value). They are still produced in the twenty first century and I have seen several politicians using them on the television.

When David finished work for the day he often found me waiting for him at Staples Corner, the junction of the North Circular and Edgware Road. I had a day off shortly after his birthday and he invited me to lunch with him at the Workmen's Café opposite the factory. Then, between sausages and mash and steamed pudding, he asked me to marry him and in that highly romantic setting I accepted and we celebrated over a cup of tea. Since then Staples Corner has changed beyond recognition, but it is a busy junction frequently mentioned on the news which makes us smile, bringing back memories of that day!

The following evening we went to Earls Court, to tell Florrie. I am sure she thought we should wait a while and did not really want to believe we were in earnest. David's parents were separated but she took it seriously enough to take us along to see his father, David senior, who was ill in hospital, so that we could tell him too. My aunts Addie and Winnie were delighted when we told them. A day or two later Dad and Anne turned up at my bedsit in their little Austin Seven. David had just arrived to take me out for the evening. We went for a drink with them at the nearby Haverstock public house, and afterwards Dad drove us back to my bedsit and before getting out of the car we told them our news. Dad was not pleased. He said he was concerned about our health, that we should both marry someone physically fit. Anne turned round in her seat and said 'David, Kathleen always said she would marry a doctor!'

Consequently we did not receive any encouragement from them to fix our wedding day.

Johnny loved the music of Beethoven, especially the Ninth Symphony: before he became a patient at Colindale he had been in the navy, and after Colindale he took a number of jobs to support his family. When we heard that he and Kathy had moved to a flat because Kathy was expecting another baby, David offered him a job as his assistant in the accountancy department at Vintens, which Johnny accepted. In those days David wore the customary uniform of office staff, a suit, with a white shirt and tie. One hot summer day Johnny turned up at the office without a tie and his boss insisted he must wear one in future. After that Johnny always did, yet they remained friends! David told me many years later, that when it came to accountancy neither of them were really competent, but they managed to get by. Both David and Johnny hated working there and stayed only long enough to find another job.

At the lack of support for our forthcoming marriage, I became very unhappy and we fell out. I packed my suit case, left my job and my bedsit and I have no idea why but I went off to live with Dad and Anne, and I began working for the Thanet school dentist. I hated being in Broadstairs and spent as much time as possible with Mary and Jim in Margate. However, I soon returned to London because David and I missed each other too much. With nowhere to live I ended up at the Young Women's Christian Association hostel in Hampstead, known as the YWCA, which provided me with a roof over my head, and bed, breakfast and evening meals, until I sorted out my life. I shared a room with three other girls who came from different parts of Great Britain.

It was a frosty morning when I went for an interview and was taken on as a secretary/ receptionist/ chairside nurse, for a dental surgeon, Dr. Perint, a middle aged Hungarian with an extremely busy NHS practice, in a large house which was also his home, opposite the Hampstead Telephone Exchange on the Finchley Road, near the underground station of that name and within downhill walking distance of the hostel. He was charming and we liked each other on sight. His home was tastefully decorated, with beautiful ornaments and sumptuously furnished with Regency furniture and a grand piano where I once heard his cousin, the classical pianist George Sandor, practising before a concert he gave in London.

However, I found working for Dr. Perint very taxing. I discussed it with Pat, a friend who was a chairside nurse in a private practice in Devonshire Place near the London Clinic. She said she was interested in the extra secretarial duties and I asked her along to meet him and we swapped jobs. I became a chairside nurse for the dentist with the private practice, who made the most wonderful gold inlays himself, on the premises, and worked there with his father and father in law (an aged American). They employed an elderly secretary who had worked there for many years. She dealt with the clerical work of all three dentists. All I had to do was look after the surgery of the junior dental surgeon, and his patients who were all well-heeled members of the aristocracy and the theatrical and political world. I put bibs round the necks of many famous people like Nancy Astor, Henrietta Tiarks, Sir Laurence Olivier, Vivian Leigh, Peter Hall, John Profumo and several American film stars. Over subsequent years when watching television I have often been heard to remark 'I put a bib round his/her neck!' While I was working there Grace Kelly married Prince Rainier and I believe several of our patients were guests at their wedding.

I remained friends with the Perint family, and David, Mando and I continued as his NHS patients. Florrie longed to return to live in Hampstead and when Malcolm and Helen Ross decided to move from 28 Primrose Hill Road, Florrie took it over and David went back home to live with her, Madeleine, and Ferg. A few weeks later he persuaded me to leave the hostel and join his family. Once more I shared a bedroom with Mando. One Saturday morning our friends Ken and Pauline called to say goodbye to David and me. They left immediately afterwards for Wales, on their motor bike.

At weekends Dad and Anne often turned up unexpectedly at Winnie and Arthur's and that summer on the way there they called unexpectedly at Primrose Hill. It was the first time that the two families had met. Madeleine was nearly fifteen and I had frequently told her how glamorous Anne was, but that day she did not live up to my description: she was wearing slacks and flat shoes which I had never seen her wear before. Florrie made them a cup of tea and after a few minutes they left for Colindale.

In July I was travelling on the top deck of a bus on the way home from work when I sensed an atmosphere similar to the one I had experienced as a child, when the second war was about to begin. All the men were reading evening newspapers full of a threatening war: our Prime Minister, Anthony Eden was sending British troops to invade Egypt and capture the Suez canal from the Egyptians, who had nationalised it; there was a short war, Britain and Israel against Egypt: there were huge demonstrations against the war in Britain and in many other countries, and the Americans forced the Allies, British and Israelis, to withdraw; Eden was obliged to resign and went to the House of Lords.

The only thing I recall about that August was that after what is known as The Glorious Twelfth the dentists I worked for were often paid in kind with a brace of game birds.

CHAPTER TWENTY THREE

The Rhine

That September David and I went on our first Continental holiday with his family. We were stupid to eat a fish supper before sailing from Dover to Ostende at night in a choppy sea and we were both sea sick. The continental trains were much cleaner than ours: every carriage had a waste basket near the toilets. We left the train in Cologne and marvelled at the cathedral which remained standing when all the surrounding buildings had been razed to the ground by the Allies during the war. From there we took a boat down the Rhine to Koblenz. The Germans were friendly and many spoke English. We enjoyed some of their food, especially wiener schnitzel and cheese cake. Every café had a clothes rack for customers' coats and a selection of daily newspapers for customers to read while imbibing coffee or beer. There was always a paper doily between cup and saucer. I had never seen such things in Great Britain. We visited Ehrenbreitstein on the opposite bank of the Rhine where I discovered Beethoven's mother was born; there we took a chair lift to the top of a small mountain overlooking the village, which gave a wonderful panoramic view of the Rhine.

While we were staying in Koblenz Mando had her first brief experience of puppy love: she met a handsome young German soldier called Hans, who clicked his heels and always politely asked on each and every occasion if he might sit with Mando at another table and always escorted her back.

We enjoyed the holiday most of all when we were left to our own devices which was most of the time. Because of his blonde hair the Germans thought David was Dutch and in restaurants we liked to submerge into the background and practise speaking German. British tourists struggling with the language mistook us for Germans, and David enjoyed teasing them but helping them with the menu. We were often amused that they wanted to eat egg and chips which was not available. Before leaving restaurants, we would pause at their tables and they would try to express their thanks; then David, never normally given to swearing, would say quietly in a clear British accent: 'The place is crawling with bloody Germans!' The look of astonishment on their faces was wonderful to behold. Our favourite tipple was a drink called dunkel beer which we discovered was normally drunk by pregnant women because of its low alcohol level but we still drank it!

On my return from holiday my boss in Devonshire Place confided to me that the ancient secretary felt I was usurping her position when I made appointments for his patients myself and he said he was in the embarrassing position of having to choose between us, for his father had made it plain that their first allegiance was to her, for she was due to retire in two years. So I left his employment and went to work for the school dentists which was fun as quite often I worked in a different location and got to know London well.

One day in October I was the last of Dr. Perint's patients for the day. After having treatment I helped Pat close the surgery and before we departed to spend the evening together we sat and talked with him. He told us how distressed he and his Hungarian patients were at the failure of the recent Hungarian Uprising when Russian tanks took over his country. He expressed his deep anxiety for his friends still living there and told us some of them had already arrived in this country as refugees; also of a friend known as The Gold King of Budapest, who together with his wife who was a scientist was hoping to come to London. Dr. Perint thought he might be able to get a position as a school dentist at Paddington General Hospital and if he turned up there would I please look after him.

My present to David for Christmas 1956 was the long playing record Songs for Swinging Lovers by Frank Sinatra. Ever since, all the songs remind us of that time when we first became swinging lovers. I helped Florrie decorate the flat for the festive season and helped with the cooking, making the mince pies and Christmas pudding.

THE YEAR 1957

Early in the new year David took a job with Pearl and Dean, a large cinema advertising agency with offices based in central London. I decided to move out of the Sinclair family home and find fresh accommodation, hoping it would prompt him to make arrangements for us to get married soon. I shared a flat with two female students, on the top floor above the shops, opposite the underground station in Belsize Park. One was a medical student and the other was studying architecture. We each had our own bedroom and shared the kitchen, bathroom and sitting room.

TERRY'S WEDDING DAY

At the end of July we went to Terry and Joan's wedding in St. Peter's church in Broadstairs. They looked radiantly happy and obviously in love. I wore an A-line dress and a large straw hat with flowers round the brim. Auntie Addie and uncle Charlie with his son Gary represented my mother's family, but auntie Mary was too busy with the summer season. We did not stay the night with Dad as he and Anne were in the process of making arrangements to emigrate to Rhodesia. Instead we met them at Winnie's the following weekend.

A couple of weeks later, Dad rang me to say that Anne would be leaving London airport the following morning. I took the Green Line bus across London to say goodbye to her but unfortunately I was too late. I found Dad in the spectators' gallery at the airport and managed to catch a glimpse of her as she boarded her flight.

In September before he sold his house Dad invited us to spend a week with him. One evening while we were there he said 'This house has never really been a home, has it?' I agreed and told him we had never been able to relax because he was too house proud. I never questioned him about the contents of the house, or how he would be disposing of them, as I coveted nothing, but now I wish I had asked him, because my mother had always wanted Terry to have her clock which was standing on the mantelpiece in the dining room. I was unaware that Terry and Dad were not on speaking terms and he sold the house and everything in it, lock stock and barrel.

DEPARTURE FOR AFRICA

On a foggy day in early December Dad arrived at my flat. David and I went for a drink with him, and afterwards he slept in my bed while I slept in our sitting room. Next morning he left for the London Docks for a ship to South Africa en route for Rhodesia. He hated flying.

Dad & Anne in Rhodesia in the sixties.

CHAPTER TWENTY FOUR

Engaged

On Christmas Eve, David and I became officially engaged. He gave me a ring with a diamond and two rubies. We went to a New Year's Eve Party and as the midnight hour approached, most unlike him and the Scottish tradition, that the first foot across the threshold should be a dark haired man, he was persuaded to do it. He disappeared just before midnight and returned a few minutes later with a piece of coal and a bottle of booze.

Cicely, my new flat mate, was a cookery student. She was nineteen years old. Her mother died when she was a very little girl. She went to spend Christmas with her father who was a widower. When she returned in the new year she danced around my room, saying as she did so, 'Something wonderful has happened! My father has married again, and not only do I have a new mother, but I have a sister, too!' I looked at her in amazement. I had never felt like that when my father met Anne. Later that week I sat down and wrote a letter to Anne, apologising for not being more welcoming when she joined our family. In reply she told me that she and Dad got married on New Year's Day.

THE YEAR 1958

I had been wearing my engagement ring for two weeks when suddenly tragedy struck. David broke off our engagement, an act he continues to say was the biggest mistake he ever made in his

David in 1957.

life. He flew to Africa to work in Ghana and Nigeria for Pearl and Dean, and I left London for Lyme Regis with a broken heart. We spent several miserable months apart, and then a long letter arrived from him followed by one every day. In June he sent me a telegram asking me to marry him: I still loved him very much and sent him a telegram saying Yes!

While he worked three months notice from Pearl and Dean he sent me money to go on a continental holiday with his mother and family. I was in Lyme Regis from April to August and during that time I worked every single day from 8:30am to 6:30 pm in a general store on The Cobb. Then I returned to Florrie in Primrose Hill, who put her arms round me, welcoming me back, and I gave thanks to God in the nearby church.

A CONTINENTAL HOLIDAY

A few days later I left with Florrie, Mando and Ferg for our continental holiday, sailing from Dover to Ostende at night and travelling by train to Aachen where we spent the day. We travelled across Germany on a night sleeper, me in the middle bunk, with Mando and Florrie above and below. They slept but I did not: at every station I heard 'Achtung! Achtung!' conjuring up memories of Hitler and the Nazi party. At Passau in the early morning we boarded a ship on the Danube, enjoying food and drink while passing many castles. Half way to Vienna we stayed overnight in a village in rooms overlooking the Danube. Mando and I went to a café on the bank and while I sat reading a long letter from David picked up at the post office there, she met a handsome young Austrian aged seventeen who could not speak English but nevertheless managed to invite her out for the evening. I agreed to act as her chaperone, but my escort was rotund like Billy Bunter. He too, could not speak English. We drank coffee, and walked along the banks of the Danube several paces behind Mando and her beau, as they stole a kiss or two. Later we said goodnight and made our way to our lodgings, to find the street in total darkness. As we stumbled towards the entrance, we heard Florrie's agitated voice from the balcony above, 'Where do you think you have been until this time of night?' It was 11.15pm and I was in my twenties! Years later we all laughed about it. Next day we boarded the ship and passed the Lorelei and more castles, arriving mid-evening in Vienna in a tremendous heat wave.

In the ten days we explored the city where I had always hoped to dance a Viennese waltz. We travelled about on the trams to see the Schönbrunn Palace, the Hofburg, St Stephen's cathedral and the open air cafés along the Danube and we went boating on the Old Danube where Mando and I took out a small yacht and Florrie and Ferg took out a canoe. On our last day there Mando and I wearing four inch stiletto heels walked with Florrie and Ferg on the outskirts of Vienna. I did not realise that we would end up on what Ferg described as 'the smallest of the Alps.' It took us all afternoon in hot sun to reach the summit and when we got there I found difficulty in breathing. We found a road as dusk began to fall, and fortunately a coach came along which Ferg stopped and it took us down into the village of Grinzing, Beethoven's birth place. A wine festival was in progress, and everyone was friendly. We spent the evening at an inn eating wiener schnitzel and drinking local wine and became somewhat intoxicated, while being serenaded by minstrels. It was enjoyable and Florrie, Mando and I got a fit of the giggles while waiting for a tram to take us back to Vienna. On board was a handsome young Viennese who thought I was Florrie's daughter. He stood before her, clicked his heels and asked her if he could marry me!

Next day we travelled across Germany by train, arriving in Cologne late in the evening and missing our connection. We visited the cathedral, had a meal and went window shopping in the city and then returned to the station which also had many shops and restaurants. Short of money, we stayed there overnight. Mando and I discovered the American Servicemen's Rest Room where we were kindly invited in and slept on comfortable settees. Next morning, after a free American breakfast, we thanked them and made our own way home without Florrie and Ferg. Mando went to stay with a school friend and I stayed with Pat at Dr Perint's home where she was acting as house keeper while he and his family were abroad.

On the Saturday night we went dancing at Kensington Town Hall. There was a live band up on the stage: we stood like wallflowers waiting to be invited to dance in a hall full of young people. The band played the hit songs of the day, making me long for David instead of strange young men. One young and handsome male asked me if he could see me again. I told him 'No! I am here tonight to keep a girl friend company; my fiancé is shortly returning from Africa.'

I returned to work at Paddington General Hospital. I worked most evenings from 7 to 9 30pm in a dental surgery in Willesden to save money to get married. One evening there an old man called to see the senior dentist, on a personal matter. I recognised him as Dr. Weisner, who had been our family doctor in Edgware: he was with my mother when she died. He looked at me long and hard, but I was too shy to introduce myself. I have always regretted it. In recent years, since going out with David, meeting hundreds of musicians, some of whom are famous, I have learnt to speak my mind more easily, becoming less shy, thank goodness!

David arrived home on Mando's birthday, Saturday October 2nd 1958. My friend Cicely had been to lunch with us. We were washing up in the kitchen when there was a knock at the front door followed by an unmistakable voice saying 'Is there any tea in the pot?' I remember exactly what I was wearing, as if it was yesterday: royal blue jeans and a multicoloured blue polo neck jumper. I opened the kitchen door to find David standing in the living room looking blonde and healthy, a guitar on one shoulder, an African bow with a quiver full of arrows on the other and surrounded by an assortment of luggage, which I later discovered included a case containing a clarinet. It was an unforgettable moment!

The next few months went by quickly. He found a new job in a Business Transfer Agency in Victoria and I continued to work at Paddington General. One day Dr Perint's Hungarian friend, a sixty year old refugee whose name was Dr Szekely, began working there. After introducing myself and an hilarious attempt to speak a few words to him in Hungarian, at the end of our working day he took me by bus to his flat in Bayswater to meet his wife who had been able to find work at Hammersmith hospital. and they told me that their son had left Hungary for England before the Uprising, and how they too had decided to flee from Budapest, leaving most of their possessions behind. While he and his wife were sitting on the train waiting to leave for Vienna Russian police came on board. Mrs Szekely was wearing a beautiful diamond ring and Dr Szekely realised there was every possibility that it would be confiscated. He had the presence of mind to take it off his wife's finger and swallow it. 'I retrieved it in Vienna,' he said with equanimity and Mrs Szekely proudly showed it to me. We became friends and he and his wife came to meet David and family one evening. Over the next two or three weeks Dr Szekely and I had lunch together in a Paddington café. It took him a long time to accept that there were no secret police in London.

CHAPTER TWENTY FIVE

The Year 1959

At the beginning of the year I helped Dr Szekely set up a NHS practice in Devonshire Street near Harley Street and worked with him until our wedding day. The wedding took place on 27th June 1959 at St Stephen's church, Rosslyn Hill, Hampstead, and was followed by a honeymoon in Cornwall, after spending our first night at the Cumberland Hotel near Marble Arch. It was the happiest day of our lives, surpassed only by the birth of our little son Malcolm almost two years later, on 10th June 1961.

The sun shone with occasional showers. Mando and Isobel, the five year old daughter of my friend Vera from Burnt Oak, were my bridesmaids and Terry gave me away. Our reception for fifty friends and a few relatives was held at the home of a friend, Pat Howell, whom I knew from the YWCA, and David's boss bought the champagne.

Johnny was Best Man and of course he and David both wore ties that day. Now, in the twenty first century, suits and ties are less common in everyday wear and David says he would not be seen dead in them, except for christenings, weddings and funerals. I often remind him that he made Johnny wear a tie at Vintens.

We have only black and white photos of our wedding. Many years later when Kathy was here in Caterham on a brief visit from Canada I showed them to her. She could not believe it when she saw that she and Johnny were present. She did not remember! I teased her saying that she drank too much champagne on our wedding day. Mando told me that she took them back to the flat on the evening of our wedding and gave them strong coffee before they made their way home on the Underground.

Whenever we talk about these events over the years, David, with a deadpan face, always tells anyone who will listen that the night before our wedding he was drunk with Johnny, that the only reason he married me was because he was drunk, and he was still drunk during the ceremony, and he was probably drugged as well. He said, many times, in front of his mother, that she always told him he should never have married me. As time went by she and I grew to love each other dearly, I called her Mum and since her passing in 1996 I grieve for her like I do for my own mother. She told me many times how happy she was to have me for a daughter in law and that she was glad to see us happily married.

David and I always say we were childhood sweethearts and even after 45 years and two lovely grandchildren we are still happy in each others' company.

INDEX OF PHOTOGRAPHS

CHAPTER ONE

CHAPTER TWO

CHAPTER THREE